PRISONER

NO

MORE

Victory After Felony

Terrell Brady

ISBN-13: 978-1727175561
ISBN-10: 1727175565

First Edition

Printed in the United States of America

Editing: Wandah Gibbs Ed. D.

Cover Art: Damian Brown

WGW Publishing Inc.
Rochester, NY

For all those who persevere regardless of the circumstances...

FOREWARD
by
TRACY L. WILLIAMS

For many of us, we discover early on that trauma seems to be woven into the fabric of our environment and pumped into our bloodstream through family, media and almost every social interaction we come across. We are cast into a world that has labeled us before we take our first breath. This sad truth however, can eventually become a blessing if correctly channeled.

In his book Terrell Brady exemplifies the fact that every stumbling block can be turned into a lesson that reinforces inner strength. As with any obstacle course used in training, you get stronger every time you overcome a challenge. This book is relatable to millions of young men across this country. It is a story of discovery, survival, and recovery.

Grit is something not everyone possesses. The mental fortitude and physical toughness required to navigate life as a young black man sets us apart from almost every individual on this planet. Grit is what every successful leader possesses.

Terrell was thought to be doomed to failure considering the amount of trauma he experienced. Having been labeled a felon, much of society had written him off and deemed him useless. But as life unfolded and with each obstacle overcome, he clearly illustrates that the willingness to learn and the willingness to change, combined with the grit instilled in us since birth, he has destroyed many long-held stereotypes.

This book will empower millions of inmates, parolees, and convicted felons. Incarceration does not equal mediocrity but instead reveals strength and perseverance. The mere act of surviving the worst that life can throw your way is proof that you can survive anything. Terrell has survived a daunting start to life with no support at home, a shaky to no support system, prison, and divorce. Yet, he has graduated college, started several businesses, and fought for his rights as a citizen.

After being told he couldn't get a passport and would never be allowed to live as a regular citizen he has shown that the same grit he was naturally born with is the same grit that sets him above all stereotypes.

You too have what it takes. Use that grit to become the person you want to be and to accomplish anything you want. This powerful book resonates with victories, strength, and leadership qualities.

Congratulations to my friend, my role model, and most importantly; my brother, for having the strength to tell his story in hopes that it will empower the millions of young men who are in the struggle. GO LEAD!!

-Tracy L. Williams

TABLE OF CONTENTS

INTRODUCTION

Growing up in extremely difficult circumstances, I did what I had to do to survive. Making sure my younger brothers, sister and I had the basic necessities and food every day became my prime motivation. Unfortunately, I eventually resorted to illegal activity in providing for my younger siblings, and the consequences of that decision have had life-long ramifications.

I've realized over the years that many, like me, have chosen a similar path and I understand that. The question becomes however; How does one navigate life following a felony conviction and incarceration? How might we prepare for reentry into the outside world?

There are many misconceptions surrounding *Returning Citizens* and what they can and cannot do. Can we vote, get a passport, work, own a business? Had I known the answer to many of these questions, my reentry would have been much easier. I now share what I've learned in hopes of helping those who come after me.

Keep in mind that there is always a better way to do things. As the saying goes, "When you know better you do better." Seek knowledge in all you do, never take anyone's word at face value, do your research and strive to become more informed today than you were yesterday.

---Terrell Brady

Chapter One

FROM PRISON TO PAVEMENT

I remember March 5, 2005 like it was yesterday, partly because my father had passed away exactly 2 weeks before, but mostly because I was finally being released from prison. I sat anxiously on my bunk that morning waiting for them to call my name. Finally, a gruff voice shouts at me, "Brady get ya shit let's go...and hurry up" I was like, "Bout damn time. Where my shit at??? Hurry up and let me the fuck up out this bitch!"

There were many times when I thought this day would never come. One day in that bitch seems like an eternity. But, now that it's here it's time to get my life back. First, I'm bout to get me some pussy. It's been two long years and if I don't get me some pussy and touch me a nice soft woman soon, I'm gonna lose my damn mind. I'm hoping my wife will come home from work and immediately get naked.

All this is running through my mind while I'm being led to the room where I'm to change out of my state greens into regular clothes. The other thing heavy on my mind is, what the hell I'm gonna eat.

I can't tell you how many times I fantasized about eating decent food. I've been eating prison garbage plates for two years now and it is certainly time to get me some real food and get my grub on. I think I'm gonna go to the

Outback Steak House and eat some prime rib and shrimp with double garlic mashed potatoes. Damn, just sitting here thinking about it is making my mouth water. You miss a lot of shit you can't get a hold of when in prison, but pussy and food are definitely at the top of my list.

Finally, the nightmare is over and I'm about to get dropped off at the train station. On the tedious bus ride to the station, everyone is talking shit to the officer. As for me I couldn't give a fuck about the cop or even saying two wasteful words to him during the ride. Made no sense to me to be quite honest. I've watched too many movies where the guy leaving prison talks junk to the prison guard only to return after doing some dumb shit or a similar crime. He then runs into the same prison guard, who tells the prisoner, "Told you I'd see you again princess." No way was I ever going to chance giving a prison guard the satisfaction of being right.

Instead of engaging in meaningless talk on the bus, I began instead to reflect on how the hell I had gotten myself into this place in life. I was like damn, I was bad as hell, though I hadn't really recognized it until that moment. While these thoughts were going through my head I remember saying to myself "Terrell it's time to get your shit together." I knew that if I didn't do things differently that it would be easy for me to fall back into old behaviors.

Finally, I made it home after a long ride on the train. I stepped off and grabbed my bags. My freedom was finally beginning to hit me, and I started grinning like a little kid opening presents on Christmas morning. I remember stretching out my arms and shouting, "I'm Free! I'm home!" Damn, I was finally experiencing something I'd anticipated for a long time, which gave me a feeling of euphoria.

I jumped into the first cab I saw and headed straight home. My wife was still at work when I arrived, but my son was home from school and let me in the house. When he opened the door and saw my face, he broke into the biggest smile I'd ever seen and said, "Hi Dad!" I was somewhat thrown off because his voice had clearly gotten much deeper over the last couple of years. I remember saying, "I see I've missed some stuff. You sound like a grown man Squirt!" He just smiled, then I gave him a big bear hug and kissed him on the cheeks. He always hated when I did that. He said, "Dad your gonna break my ribs your squeezing me too tight." I laughed and said, "I'm sorry Squirt it's just that I missed you."

Just seeing my son's face made me realize how much I truly had missed him. Soon after my arrival, my daughter came home from school. I was upstairs when she arrived, and I could hear my son telling her I was home. She ran straight upstairs to her room to find me standing there and screamed, "Dad!" Then ran towards me and gave me a huge hug and said, "I missed you!" "Hey Shrimp, I missed you too!"

I sat and chatted with the kids until my wife came home. I needed time to be alone with them. They were now a couple of years older and better able to understand what was going on. So, I attempted to explain where I had been and why. They sat and listened and made a few comments. They both asked me why I hadn't told them before I left what was going on and I let them know that I didn't think they were at an age where they could fully understand. My arrest was not something I was proud of.

Then, my son said some profound things that had me rethink his ability to understand complex and difficult situations at a young age. He began by saying,

"Dad I know what you were doing was wrong and we figured out where you had to be once a couple of weeks had passed. Mom would often cry herself to sleep at night because you were not home. I used to ask her why she was upset, and she wouldn't tell me anything, then I would ask her when you were coming home, and she'd cry even more. I also had figured out what you must've been up to because you had all this time to take me and my sister to school in the mornings and pick us up from our after-school activities. You would be at all the games but for some reason you always had money and I hardly ever saw you go to work. You went to work for a little while then not again for a long time."

I was dumbfounded by what he was saying, but I allowed him to continue because I was curious...

"I understand and respect your choice Dad because I saw how hard you tried to get a job and always noticed how much pressure you were under. You were helping others out doing things for your brothers and taking care of all of us too."

Once he'd finished talking I was amazed by everything he'd said. "Squirt I am by no means proud of the choices I made because it took me away from all of you, for two whole years. I can never get those years back, and by no means do I want to teach you that what I did was ok because it was not. I hated every minute of it. The entire time, I was wishing I could find something else to do, despite my asthma.

We finished our conversation just around the time my wife would be coming home from work. I jumped in the shower to wash off what felt like two years' worth of jail time when suddenly I heard the door open, then the shower curtain being pulled back. It was my wife! She just grinned, and said, "Hi," as she leaned in to give me a kiss. She stood there for a moment then began talking to me about dinner, but not before I tried to convince her to jump in the shower with me. She was like "Boy stop, the kids are up, and they are just as excited to see you as I am. Let's wait until later tonight and in the meantime, let's go to Outback Steakhouse for dinner. I'm sure that's what you want. I just chuckled and said, "And how do you know this?" Before she left the bathroom, she leaned in for another kiss and said, "I'm happy your home."

After dinner and a quick trip around my old stomping grounds, it was time for bed. I was thinking, it was about time, because I was about to explode. The kids finally got off to bed and then it was our turn. I jumped in the shower again (because I could), then stepped out with nothing on but my towel. She did the same and that's when we got it on. I finally, got everything I wanted that day, which was, some decent food and some pussy!

The following day I called my friend Deek as soon as I got home from the parole office. My wheels began to spin as I knew I had no money and was curious as to what Deek had been up to while I was inside. Deek swung by my house and picked me up to go grab some lunch. I asked him what he had been up to because I needed to make a few bucks. After I said that, he looked at me like I was crazy and said, "Rell, you're on parole. If I give you some work, that would mean I'm not a true friend. Complete your parole, then we can discuss it." I developed a new respect for him that day as anyone else would've simply put the work in my hand and not tried to encourage me to leave it alone for the time being. We finished lunch then he dropped me off at home. I had a lot on my mind and was really worried about what I was gonna do next?

Shortly after the excitement of being home came had subsided, I signed up for classes at Bryant & Stratton College, and decided to major in Accounting and Business Administration. I made honor roll every semester I attended. I graduated from Bryant and Stratton in May of

2007 and at graduation, I received the *Award of Excellence* in Accounting for outstanding academic performance.

Being recognized for my efforts and hard work was a first for me. It was something I was not used to as I had always felt invisible and overlooked no matter how hard I worked or how much effort I had put into something. To be recognized during graduation in front of tons of people, made me feel as though I had finally accomplished something worthwhile.

Once the celebrations were over and the euphoria of graduation had worn off I figured it was probably time to get a job. To gain some much-needed experience, I found a couple of internships. My first one was in the accounting department of an architectural firm. I was hoping that upon completion of the internship I'd become a permanent part of the team. I worked hard and learned the content and company culture.

I did this for six months and when my internship was coming to an end, I sat down with my boss to discuss my performance. She told me how wonderfully I had done and how much of an asset I had been during my time there. She told me I'd helped considerably with the transition to their new accounting software system and how everyone recognized that without my help it would have taken the department much longer to implement. She then proceeded to tell me that unfortunately there was no room in their current budget to hire me but would keep me in mind once they were able to bring on extra staff. This news bummed me out because I had hoped this would be my opportunity to land a job in my field of study straight out of college.

After my first internship I completed a second one at a marketing firm. I didn't enjoy it as much, but once again thought it might be my opportunity to get a foot in the door and navigate my way to full-time work. Once again, upon completion of my six-month internship, I was told there was no room for me in the company. Obviously, this was extremely frustrating, and I knew I had to figure something out soon. My student loans had now run out and it was time to earn money, so I could pay the household bills.

Naturally I couldn't expect my wife to carry me much longer and I thought perhaps I should start my own business. I decided to research small businesses that require very little startup money. Lawn care services seemed to be a front runner and I decided to try my hand at it. I already had some lawn care equipment and a pick-up truck at my disposal and figured I could upgrade equipment as needed.

With renewed enthusiasm I commenced to make this venture a reality. To make it official I went downtown to register my business and obtain a tax ID number. Next, I obtained liability business insurance as I didn't want to get caught out there uninsured and risk being sued. Everything was coming together and now it was time to network and comb the city for business. It wasn't long before I secured my first set of contracts and began doing lawncare for a property management company. How I come to acquire my first multi-property contract was through my long-time friend, Deek, who also hired me to maintain the properties that he owned. I'd say it's always good to look within your own network as you may be surprised at what opportunities may come from it.

This venture lasted for two years and I did quite well financially, at least well enough to contribute to the household expenses, pay my taxes, and add to my savings. Unfortunately, during that time, I had very little support at home and my asthma reared its ugly head. Though I had hired two guys to help me out, they proved to be unreliable which put the bulk of the work back on me. I ended up burning out and being sick all the time. Unfortunately, for health reasons I had to give up the lawn care business.

Again, I needed to find something I could do before I ran through my savings, so I decided to take a civil service exam as I'd heard the post office was hiring. Upon arrival to the examination room, I was a little anxious as I knew this wasn't a typical test.

Once the proctor had passed out the exam he told the class he had a few house cleaning items to go over before we began. First, he wanted to make sure everyone was indeed there to take the civil service exam for the post office position. Next, he asked the class if there were any people there who had been convicted of a felony or who had felony charges pending. Then he proceeded to tell us that a felony conviction would disqualify us from taking the test and applying for the position. My jaw dropped, and I was thoroughly embarrassed when myself and several others had to get up and leave the room. My past was beginning to haunt me.

Chapter Two

HOW THE HELL DID I GET HERE?

I wasn't really a bad guy per se, I had just done some bad guy things, but those things were usually out of necessity. I can remember a time during my last years in high school where I had dreams and goals and wanted to join the service or become a firefighter.

I just knew my life after high school was going to be so much better than it had been growing up. I didn't always run the streets and hustle. It just so happened that because of the detours in my life this is where I landed. I had wanted better for myself and even attempted to do right in terms of employment and education, and yet for some reason, nothing seemed to work out for me no matter how hard I tried.

My life has essentially been a roller coaster ride, and I wish I could change much of it. They say that what happens in a person's childhood is what makes or shapes that person. Though it does not have to dictate the outcome of a person's life, it certainly had a profound impact on mine.

I've often asked myself if I'd ever been happy as a child and I can honestly say without hesitation that I was not! I never got to just enjoy being a kid. I couldn't do many of the things my friends were doing because I had to babysit my siblings or work to help provide for my family.

11

When I did go out with friends I had to be home much earlier than the other kids.

I tried not to think too much about the difficult things that took place growing up but found it to be a challenge. Every now and then bad memories would flood my mind like explosives going off in my head. I'd snap out of it then think to myself, "What the Fuck! Why am I thinking about this shit?" It took years for me realize I had never dealt with any of the traumatic things from my past. I thought it was better to suppress my feelings and just act as if none of it ever happened.

Try as I might to make a life for myself, I kept getting stuck and couldn't seem to get over the hump. I was young and had a whole life ahead of me, yet I felt as though I didn't have much of a life at all. Of course, I knew I wasn't the only one to go through trials, but people need to understand that the stacks against some of us are higher than for others. And, it can be especially difficult to keep moving in the right direction after you've had a felony conviction.

At this point, I had no idea how to proceed nor whom to talk to for advice in successfully navigating the various obstacles in my life. Because of this and other factors, I found it easier to simply go back to what I knew best, *the hustle.*

Chapter Three

GENERATIONAL CURSE

A generational curse had begun in my family structure within my grandparent's home. The dysfunction had been passed on to them from their parents and of course now to their children. I grew up in a quiet, peaceful country town in Upstate New York where everyone knew each other. Granted, I had both a mom and a dad in the home so at first glance, you might think we had a typical, traditional household. This couldn't have been farther from the truth. Looking back now, I realize we were the poster family for generational dysfunction instead.

Later in life, both my grandparents found God and learned to live well-rounded, spiritually based, and wholesome lives. Unfortunately, much damage had already been done. By then, my grandparent's children were now adults raising their own children. Though on many occasions I witnessed my grandparents offering advice to my parents, aunts, and uncles; no one listened. Instead of taking much needed advice, they simply continued whatever behaviors my grandparents were now trying to correct.

It took years of trial and error, but my grandparents eventually figured out a recipe for sustaining their marriage and wielding influence on their children and their children's children. This was clearly displayed when they gained custody of one of their grandchildren. I must say, I applaud them because throughout their lifetime they never stopped striving to become better people. No matter how much they endured, they fought to improve themselves and it showed in their actions and deeds.

My grandfather was a good man and I secretly wanted to emulate him and make him proud of me. He was the head of the family, a church deacon, and a Mason. He regularly attended meetings and I found myself wondering what went on there. I was not privy to any of that information because I was just a child, plus I never worked up the nerve to ask. If I had asked however, he probably would have sat me down and explained it to me the best he could without divulging too much about this brotherly organization. It is because of my grandfather that later in life, I too became a Mason. I am continuing my grandfather's legacy and thank him often for leading the way. Joining the Masons was one of the best decisions I ever made because it helped me strive to become a better man.

My Grandmother was the sweetest woman you ever met. She devoted herself to her family. I loved being around her and loved her energy. She was an amazing cook and whenever I went to the house the first thing I said when I walked through the door was, "Hi Grandma what you make?" She would just chuckle and grin at me. She'd tell me to go into the kitchen to see what was in there. I loved coconut cake and hers was so moist and delicious that it melted in your mouth. In fact, just thinking about it now is making my mouth water and I can almost taste it. I remember my mother telling me not to get a slice of cake and my grandmother responding, "Let him get some, there's plenty, he can have as much as he wants. Heck if he doesn't eat it it's just gonna go to waist. It's only me and ya father in the house now and he sure don't need to be eating all that cake."

Boy I sure do miss her, and I miss going to visit her. Her house was full of love all the way around. I remember going to see my grandparents and not wanting to go back home at all. In the back of my mind I kept thinking, "Please leave me here... please! I don't want to go back home." Given the choice I would absolutely have stayed at my grandparent's.

Chapter Four

THE FALLOUT

Though I didn't begin to realize it until I'd reached adulthood, the more I reflected on my childhood, the more I realized how much the violence at home had affected me. It's sad to say, but the brightest child full of potential is completely diminished when brought up in the wrong environment. Choices are lessened, your thought processes change, the type of people you look up to shifts, and your perception of the world and the people in it becomes completely skewed.

For me, trust was something that had to be earned. I never trusted anyone upon meeting them and always felt they had ulterior motives. In the back of my mind my thoughts would wander, and I would ask myself, "Why does this person want to befriend me?" What do I have that they want. Many times, my intuition was correct. Turns out many guys only wanted to become my friend, so they could meet my sister. This was the story of my life throughout middle and high school. It got to where I didn't even want to attend the same school as her!

Growing up, my sister and I were very close nonetheless. We were each other's primary support system within the house which we referred to as *our private hell*. Although we were close I didn't want to hang out with her all the time because I knew she would do things to get us in trouble and I also knew I'd get the

16

blame for it. Any mischief that warranted a whooping, my father would inflict on me.

He used to justify it by saying I was the oldest and therefore should've known better and be able to tell her right from wrong. I must say I did not agree this should be the case considering we are only two years apart. It's not like I'm five or ten years older than her. We were always given the same instructions at the same time in the same manner. I started to believe she got a kick out of seeing me punished for her dirty deeds. It wasn't her fault and it was my father's poor parenting that resulted in my being beaten, but as a child, I hated it and began to resent my sister for it as well.

When I was 10 years old, we suddenly gained an addition to the family: a little brother, then a year later my youngest brother was born. They were very close, so close that people often mistook them for twins.

By the time they were of school age my parents were too busy partying to take care of our needs, let alone the two youngest. I was forced to take on the role of caretaker. I had no idea what I was going to do but instinctively knew I needed to make sure our basic needs were met. To ensure we ate daily, I went to work. I got my first job at the age of 13 as a rent-a-kid. I worked for an agency that sent kids to peoples' homes to do odd jobs for them. I mostly got calls from the elderly. It wasn't such a bad gig considering they not only paid me, but they also fed me, gave me goodies, and sometimes sent me home with gifts.

Unfortunately, my parents snatched my money from me the moment I walked through the door. And although they purchased some food, the balance was used on their recreational activities. When I turned 14 I began working at McDonalds which was better for us as I knew I could take food home with me at the end of my shift so at least my sister and little bros could eat. A year later my sister began working at the same McDonalds, which increased the amount of food coming into the house. One thing didn't change however, our parents still seized our wages the moment we came home with our paychecks.

At 16, I started working at KFC, which afforded me a lot more perks. I brought home complete meals even on the days I didn't work. I got paid more than at McDonalds and the management staff taught me many things. I learned how to cash my own checks, which enabled me to keep more of the money I made, thus giving less of it to my parents. At last I could buy my own clothes, and provide small Christmas and birthday presents for my siblings.

Although I was still in school full-time, I worked every hour they allowed me to. For years, my parents continued pissing away all the money they could get their hands on and things went on like this until I was old enough to make my own decisions.

I got so fed up with my parent's behavior that I asked my friend JB if I could room with him. Thankfully he agreed to take me in as a roommate though I felt bad leaving my little brothers and sister at home to deal with the mess my parents had created. I just couldn't take it any longer. The beatings, not having any money because it was being taken from me by my parents, watching my little brothers being neglected, my sister not being taught things a mother should teach her daughter, the drinking and drugging, the fighting, and all the uncertainty had become just too much.

This was not a life I wanted to continue living. Though my situation improved, I always wished that I'd had enough money to take my siblings with me. If we could've lived somewhere together without our parents, we would have had a much better time of it. To this day I wonder what life would have been like if I had been able to do this, thus leaving our parents to fend for themselves.

Leaving the house did prove to be best for me because I was still able to graduate from high school while working full-time.

Chapter Five

ARE YOU KIDDING ME?

One day, out of nowhere, my mother and father pulled me to the side to say they had something they needed tell me. The way they approached me was out of the ordinary and based on their tone of voice, whatever it was, sounded serious. I started wracking my brain to figure out what was going on or what I'd done wrong that I'd forgotten about.

They led me into the kitchen and told me to have a seat at the table. I sat down while my mother stood near me, and my father sat at the opposite end of the table. The reason they wanted to talk to me was to tell me that my *father* was not actually my *father*. My mother was indeed my mother, but the person I had called father for the last 16 years, was not my dad.

Turns out, the man I'd called father all my life, had begun a relationship with my mother shortly before I was born. He married her when I was about three months old. They agreed that he would adopt me, I would take his last name, and he would raise me as his own. After hearing this bombshell, my emotions flooded me with intense anger and hurt. All I could think of was, not only had the last 16 years of my life been a living hell, my entire life had been a lie.

Obviously, my next thought was, who the hell is my real father and why am I just learning about him now? Here I am, a 16-year old boy sitting with two adults I've always referred to as my parents, but one was not! Just then, my mother proceeds to tell me who my biological father is. She even offers to share information with me on how to contact him if I should choose to.

At this point, I am completely numb and have no idea how to react to the news. I can't quite determine if I'm angry, shocked or all of the above. I know this much, I am at a complete loss for words. Then they have the nerve to ask me if I have any questions. Of course, I had a shitload of questions, but instead I just got up from the table with no idea what to say or do.

Later, once the dust had settled, I was able to reflect on what they had told me, and I decided to write a letter to the person who was apparently my real father. Some time passed, but a response I did not get.

Eventually, when I was 21 years old, my aunt and cousin arranged to have me meet my fraternal grandfather. Until then, I had no interaction with any of my biological family except my cousin's father. He had graciously begun building a relationship with me as soon as he'd found out where I was. Turns out my cousin's father and my biological father are brothers, and that our mothers are twin sisters.

Anyway, on the day I went to meet my grandfather we drove for about an hour to reach the small town in upstate N.Y. where I was born. As we pulled up to the house I saw three gentlemen standing in the driveway. I got out of the car to say hello. The gentlemen introduced themselves one after the other. There, standing before me were Pop-Pop my grandfather, my uncle, and most surprisingly; my biological father! So, there you have it, that was how and when I met him. I stood there in utter shock as no one had mentioned he might be there.

Dazed, I wondered if this was really happening or if I was just day dreaming. The man I'd been told was my real father was standing right there in front of me. I had no idea how to react. I thought about ignoring him like he had my letters, and just addressing my grandfather and uncle instead. Then I thought I should maybe lay into him with a good tongue lashing, but decided it wasn't worth the energy, so I just kept my cool.

I spoke and said hello to everyone. My grandfather put his arm around me and took me into the house to meet my grandmother. He said, "Terrell this is your grandmother, Madear." I said hello and gave her a hug. She said, "Oh baby it is so nice to finally meet you." At that moment I wanted to spazz out and say, "You had 21 years' worth of opportunities to meet me what the fuck are you talking about?" But instead I said nothing.

He then introduced me to my aunt, who also hugged me. I was beginning to wonder if all this was genuine? Why on earth had my grandfather finally *summoned me*? Is there something going on with his health? Had a conversation about me recently come up between him and my biological father? Or was this simply my grandfather's way of bringing my father and I together? I was extremely curious because so many years had passed with *ZERO* contact with any of them. So why now?

Now that all the formalities were out of the way the awkward silence began. I had no idea what to say to anyone because I didn't know them, and as I recall, they also sat silent trying to figure me out. My cousin, who essentially set all this in motion by arranging the meeting, was the only one talking, which helped break the silence. It was easier for her because she knew more about the family as she had occasionally interacted with several of them.

During all the chatter I took the opportunity to take a good look at my *father* to see if I resembled him in any way. I believe I look more like my mother than I do him. I don't have his height, skin complexion, nothing that I saw. Others tell me I look like him, but I guess it's open to interpretation. I did notice that his build and mine are similar, but hey what does that really mean?

The moment came when my *father* asked me to join him outdoors, so we could have a moment alone to talk. I remember walking outside to the porch and standing by the stairs. I felt like running because my emotions were all over the place and I was unsure of what might blurt out of my mouth. I was bitter to say the least.

He then proceeded to ask me questions about myself. After a little of the *tell me about yourself* part of the conversation I began to ask him some tough questions, the ones I *really* wanted answers to. Honestly, I could care less about the small talk everyone had been sharing since I'd stepped out of the car. I asked, "Where you been all these years and why on earth am I just now getting to meet you?" His response was, "I currently live in New Jersey and have been there for some time now. So that's where I been. I don't get to travel to Upstate New York much."

Then I asked him if he'd received the letters I'd mailed him five years ago. He told me he never received any letters from me and that if he had he would have written me back. To be quite honest I was unsure whether to believe him or not. I thought to myself that it was certainly plausible that my mother had never mailed the letters, but at this point heaven only knew what the truth was?

Next, I asked him why he never tried to contact me considering his brother, my uncle, knew where I was and that it would've been easy for him to get my contact information. He responded by saying, "Back when you were first born your mother, your *father*, and I had a conversation, and we decided together that he would raise you and take care of you as his own and that I wouldn't

24

interfere with that decision because they were getting married. I didn't want to be the cause of a failed marriage simply because your dad was threatened by the thought of me pursuing your mother." My jaw dropped because no one had told me this part of the story. I just assumed he wanted nothing to do with me for one reason or another and honestly, I still felt that way. After all, so much time had passed and though I was now an adult, there had been no communication or any attempt at making himself known to me.

As he was talking away, I couldn't help but think to myself, here comes more bullshit. He told me that since we'd finally met we should exchange information and that he would stay in touch going forward. Still stinging from confusion and anger, as soon as he said this I immediately responded with, "Listen I am a grown ass man now with a child of my own. I'm not some snotty nose little kid who is sitting in the window waiting for his daddy to show up. If you choose to stay in touch with me that is totally your call since you now have my information. The ball is in your court but believe me when I tell you that I won't be waiting around, nor will I be burning up your phone line, trying to reach out to you."

Soon after this conversation my aunt, cousin, and I got ready to leave. We said our goodbyes, got in the car, and started up the driveway towards the road. I thought to myself that I would wait and see how this all played out.

After all, I felt I had given him an in, instead of completely shutting him out like others may have.

I didn't hear from him again until his daughter, my sister, passed away. Yes, *My Sister* you heard right. Something my father forgot to mention during our first encounter. How the hell he gonna forget to mention that he has another child? This is something I can't fathom yet he made no mention of her at all. Just another strike against him in my eyes.

My cousin is the one who called me to tell me what happened as she had received the information first. So, I rode to New Jersey where again I was surrounded by family, though they were essentially still strangers to me. It felt awkward being introduced to people during a time of grief, but I guess there would have been no other time for me to meet everyone.

I should point out that my *father* was not the one making the introductions, instead it was my uncle and my cousin who did. Without these two I would simply have been a lost soul in the crowd and would have never found out who was who. During the funeral he and I didn't interact much, and I didn't press the issue. When it was time to leave I just left.

Realizing that things hadn't really picked up between the two of us I didn't expect a relationship would ever blossom and it really never did. Over the years I have spoken to him a few times on the phone. He has called me a handful of times over my entire life and I have called him a few more. People say some relationships are just not meant to be, especially if you must chase after them.

When I was a child and first learned of my biological father it bothered me, but as I became an adult it didn't so much. I just made up my mind that I would never do this to any children of mine. For this reason and to the best of my ability, I have been an active parent throughout my children's lives. This was one generational curse that would cease with me.

Chapter Six

MY NORMAL WAS NOT THE NORM

It took me many years and a variety of experiences to fully understand that what I had learned while growing up was all wrong. Along the way I met families who did things much differently than ours did, which is how I began to discover my *normal* was not the norm. I often went to my childhood friends' homes where I soon began to realize how different their lives were compared to mine.

Conner and Justin were Caucasian friends of mine with whom I would sometimes spend the night and where I was occasionally invited to stay for dinner. Whenever I entered their homes I was greeted by an adult. Often, I was asked to go wash up as dinner was about to be served. Upon entering the dining room, my friend's mom would gently invite me to take a seat at the dining room table. I remember saying, "Mrs. Norton are you sure you have enough? I don't want to take away from anyone." She would say, "Nonsense, have a seat so we can pray."

When sitting down to enjoy a well-prepared meal, I was distinctly aware of the contrast between this household and mine. In our house, not only did we not sit down to dinner together, but open conversation during dinner was nonexistent. The more I visited their homes, the closer we all became, and they treated me as part of their extended family. I remember whenever we walked into Conner's house after school, his mom would greet us and ask how our day had gone. No one ever asked me that at my house.

My friend Justin regularly went to tutoring, took archery lessons, and he and his family went on vacation every summer. I didn't know the first thing about archery let alone what a yearly vacation looked like. I was lucky if we even drove to another part of New York state.

The other stark difference between their homes and mine was the way their parents interacted with each other. The mom and dad were loving and affectionate towards each other and the children. Affection was something my family never displayed, and you certainly never saw men showing other men affection, whether they were family or not.

I now know the contrast between my home and theirs was not primarily a Black-White thing, but more of a value thing. The other families valued their children and each other. They valued their homes and kept them clean and orderly. Don't get me wrong my mother made sure our home stayed clean in the literal sense, but the fighting and arguing is what made for a chaotic environment. Other families seemed to value the experiences had at school and their children's friends. But as for my parents they made sure we stayed on top of our school work or that would be another reason for some sort of punishment. My parents didn't place much value in the whole schooling experience. We would have opportunities presented to us like field trips and after-school activities but could rarely take advantage of them. And as for our friends my parents didn't take the time to get to know them or their parents for that matter. I've since met plenty of black families who model the same behavior I saw at my friends' houses but growing up I thought Blacks lived one way and Whites another. Nothing is that cut and dry because financial stability, kindness, love, helpfulness, and patience come in many colors. Today, my own home is one where I strive to value each person living there. Where we have solid, open conversations, lots of LOVE, laughter, and joy and we also take the time to pour into one another and build each other up.

In the same way that my grandparents learned to operate within a distinct set of morals and practices, human beings always have choices. One choice I've determined to make is to continue evolving for as long as I live. Learning new things, trying new ideas, not being afraid to take risks, reading biographies, surrounding myself with good people and those that will challenge me whenever necessary. All these strategies have contributed to growth and learning in my life. Thankfully, the family we are born into does not have to dictate our outcome in life and I am so glad that the life I led as a child is far removed from the life I live today...

Chapter Seven

TRYING TO FIT IN

School was not an especially wonderful experience for me and I remember being this awkward, shy kid who didn't have many friends. I felt as though I never fit in. I discovered I liked music however and began to focus my energies there. I played drums and all other percussion instruments and I became good at it. I made the band and participated in many concerts and marching band events. They say finding a passion is the very beginning of developing grit and is also what helps a person persist during the difficult stages in life.

Though I enjoyed playing the drums and participating in band concerts, drum corps, jazz band, and the marching band, I still felt empty and alone because my family did not come to support me. My father never came to any of my performances and the only reason my mother appeared once or twice, was so she wouldn't have to come back later to pick me up. I was just a kid, but more times than not, I had to find my own way to and from events.

I saw other parents congratulating their children and celebrating their performances. At every event, I looked out into the audience hoping to see someone from my family, but they were rarely, if ever there. Seeing a familiar face in the crowd, would have made me feel valued. It really sucked always feeling alone in the world, let alone within my own family.

Other than the band, I never really felt like I was a part of anything or anyone. In fact, there were many days I said to myself, "I bet if I went missing today no one would even notice I was gone." Or, "If I hadn't been born, what difference would it have made to the world?" My feelings of insignificance were so strong that at times I behaved recklessly, not caring how dangerous my actions were. I was beginning to not value my own life.

My band teacher was my go-to guy and although I never said anything to him about my dysfunctional home life he seemed to have known there was something going on. I was the only kid in the class who always distanced himself from the crowds and commotion. Now that I think about it maybe my band teacher was acting as my safety net. He never shooed me away, never asked me to leave his room, even if he knew I was skipping a class or if he had a class going on at the time. He didn't even pressure me to talk or tell him why I was always in his class when I wasn't supposed to be. I could come in and just be part of the class. I was grateful to him for that and the music room became my safe-haven.

I looked forward to band class every day and even when I didn't have class that day, I went anyway. Teachers should never underestimate the influence they have on their students. They may not realize it at the time, but a kind word of encouragement goes a long way in the life of a young person, particularly if they are not receiving what they need at home. I will forever be grateful for Mr. Grantham.

Chapter Eight

MONEY MATTERS

We should have been in a very good place financially. My father was a Tool & Die maker who earned good money and my mother worked at a factory. She didn't earn as much as he did but brought in a decent paycheck nonetheless. Our bills were menial because we lived in subsidized housing in the Doran Projects. They didn't have any credit card debt and my father only bought used cars, so he could avoid having a car note. I only remember one exception when my maternal grandmother helped my mother purchase a sparkly new white Chevette. I remember this vividly because it was the car in which I learned to drive.

Since both my parents worked and we had very little expenses and no debt, we should have been doing well financially. Instead, what I witnessed was my parents partying all their money away, then borrowing money to get through the rest of the week. When they got paid they'd have to return all the money they'd borrowed from friends and family and the cycle would begin again. This behavior resulted in an endless spiral of debt recovery.

Their poor money management left us children wondering if this was how life was meant to be. In no way did they teach us kids anything about managing money. What we learned instead, was how to live from paycheck to paycheck and how to borrow what you needed from someone else. I didn't know what a bank account was because I never saw my folks go to a bank. Instead, they cashed their checks at check cashing places, who charged money to use their services.

When I finally got a job of my own, I followed in my parent's footsteps and did the same thing for a very long time. Sad to say, I just didn't know any better. Proper money management was obviously not taught in school nor in our house. You essentially just winged it and hoped for the best.

Every year, my parents waited for their income tax return to make large purchases, instead of using the money to catch up on bills or establish some sort of savings or emergency account. When comparing other neighborhood households, it appeared that we weren't the only ones that operated this way.

Learning the basics of money management and financial planning is desperately needed and should be taught in grade school. Everyone I associated with seemed to have the same mindset when it came to money. No one had a savings account, no one knew how to balance a checkbook, and many didn't have a bank account of any type.

Every household should understand and know the basics of money management. Learning the concept of saving and not living beyond one's means would have been nice. But it wasn't until later in my adult life did I learn this strategy. I believe that it was because of going without and constantly scrimping for basics, that once I learned some basic principles. I decided I would never allow myself to get into the same financial trouble my parents were always in and that I would always keep a savings account. You just never know what emergency may occur. In planning ahead and taking steps to prepare for the future, it prevents you from going into debt or needing to borrow money.

As I write this I am reminded how we as a community tend to not purchase life insurance for ourselves, our children or the elders in our families. Not doing so often leaves the burden of funeral expenses on the closest family members, which can be costly. It is my belief that it's unfair to burden those left behind with that expense. Losing someone is emotionally taxing and having to make funeral arrangements during a time of grief is difficult enough. Having to figure out how to finance the funeral can be a whole other animal. The cost can be enormous between the funeral as well as clearing up debt or bills accumulated during the person's lifetime. Everything costs so why not prepare for this expense ahead of time. As the saying goes, "Poor planning on your part don't make for an emergency on mine."

It saddens me that I was not taught this in my younger years, and that there wasn't a policy in place when my father passed away. If there had been, burying him would not have presented such a huge financial strain on the family. Everyone had to come together just to cover the expenses. This is one generational mishap that ceased to continue after my father's generation. I've made sure to secure a policy for myself and have discussed this practice with my daughter as well.

There are many inexpensive policies available today. When exploring those options, make sure to review the various types that exist. The main two life insurance policy options are; *term life*, which is really a life insurance policy you're renting. Once the term comes, the policy is terminated, but it is generally a less expense option. Also, you cannot borrow against this type of policy. The other type is *whole life*, which is a life insurance policy you pay into that builds equity over time and allows you to borrow against it. It's somewhat like borrowing from yourself. I look at it as a glorified savings account. Likewise, it's a way of passing down wealth from generation to generation, depending on the policy's worth. Never-the-less, either option is worth the investment. I have an active policy because I refuse to leave the burden of my funeral expenses on my family.

It's easy to explore your options with an insurance agent. They will meet with you free of charge. If you can only afford term life insurance at first, go with that. Eventually, you should be able to buy a whole life insurance plan. Either way, it is a very important life step.

Chapter Nine

FROM BAD TO WORSE

Meanwhile, not only was my father abusing alcohol, he began using other substances which further altered his mood. Instead of getting wasted mostly on weekends, he started using every day, which made living at home that much more unbearable. This meant more violent outbursts, and because of his new drug habit, he was spending a lot more money.

Financing his drug and alcohol habit often left us suffering without food, lights, and heat and resulted in us being on the verge of eviction several times. Going without the very basic necessities never felt good, but the thought of being homeless was the absolute worst.

I often wondered why all this was happening and asked myself if I were somehow being punished. What on earth was I alive for? To endure pain and suffering? Was this how life was meant to be? I had so many questions but very few answers. All I knew is that I wanted things to improve and quickly.

Though I knew the circumstances of my life were beyond my control, there were times when I couldn't help feeling that I wanted my life to end. I knew it was getting bad because I remember the day I called myself attempting suicide. I really didn't know what I was doing but thought I would try anyway. Mimicking something I'd seen in a movie, I turned on the gas stove and the oven. I blew out the pilot lights and just let the gas run. I sat in a chair I'd pulled close to the stove and even shoved my head inside the oven a few times. I was home alone and didn't expect anyone for an hour or more. I sat there for some time and felt a little light headed but nothing more.

My mother was the first one through the door and asked me why the house smelled like gas. I lied and told her I was trying to cook something and had turned on the stove, but that the pilot light was out. All the while I'm thinking what if my mother didn't get home when she did would I have succeeded? Was my mother divinely sent there at that moment to stop me during this potentially tragic event? Hmmm... more questions. As she's rushing over to check the stove she calls out, "Boy are you trying to kill everybody!" In my head I was like, *not everybody, just me*! But of course, I didn't say a word.

Since my suicide attempt hadn't succeeded, as soon as I was old enough to leave the house, I stayed away as much as possible instead. Eventually however, I had to return and with each time the following questions nagged at me: Wasn't there something better in store for me and if so, when would it reveal itself?

Chapter Ten

VIOLENCE, A WAY OF LIFE

My father was the antithesis of a good role model. He became violent each time he drank, which was often. After every drinking episode he would come home and beat my mother, then he would turn his anger towards me. There were many nights where my father came home after a night of drinking and beat me right out of my sleep. My mother tried to intervene from time to time but this would just enrage my father even more and the beating would become more intense.

I remember one night, when he hit me so hard that he knocked me clear across the room and into the wall. Another time, out of the blue, he decided he would take me fishing. He rarely fished with me but knew that I loved it and that I enjoyed going down to the river especially with my grandparents. Riding in the car towards our destination, and excited to be going on a fishing trip, I opened the container of spikes and asked my dad "What are these?" He just flipped out. He started beating me in the head while he was driving. To this day I don't know why he got so upset with me...

One day, I got suspended from school for fighting on school grounds. I was defending my sister from a boy that wouldn't stop picking on her and hitting her. Once I got home my father was not back from work yet, but my mother was there waiting on me because the principal had called to inform her of the incident. After talking to my mother and giving her the entire story, she decided not to punish me because she believed the action I took was justified. I was relieved that my mom understood the situation and was hoping she could sway my father with the same explanation I'd given her.

When my father finally walked through the door, he seemed to be in a relatively good mood. Thankfully, it appeared he hadn't stopped anywhere to toss a few back before coming home. After he got settled I heard him call my name, "TERRY," which is what he called me, "Come downstairs." I hurried down to see what he wanted. He proceeded to say, "Ya momma told me what happened today at school." I answered, "Yes." Terrified, because I was already imagining how this conversation might end... My father then says, "Well we will discuss it after dinner, once you've taken your bath and are getting ready for bed." I said, "OK," and ran out of the room feeling as though I'd just escaped death.

Later that evening after my bath, as promised, my father comes into my room. While I'm still drying off, he proceeds to whoop me with his belt. Standing naked and wet, the pain was unbearable. If you've ever had a whooping butt naked it's bad but add wet skin to that equation and it's horrendous.

As he dished out the ass whoopin, each hit was accompanied by a word. The beating sounded something like this; "Don't! (slap) You! (slap) Ever! (slap) Have! (slap)

The! (slap) School! (slap) Call! (slap) Here! (slap) Telling! (slap) Us! (slap) You! Been! In! A! Fight! Ever! Again! I Don't care what the reason is!" Meanwhile, I'm crying and trying to keep it together while attempting to explain, "Ok Dad... Ok Dad... But Dad, I was only trying to help my sister because a boy was hitting her." He then yells, "SHUT UP! I DIDN'T TELL YOU TO SAY ANYTHING!" Because he was yelling at me the entire time, he started to lose his voice and the screaming eventually lessened in intensity.

I received this type of punishment for years. I couldn't go an entire week without getting an ass whoopin for one reason or another. At one point I started to believe I was on earth to be his human punching bag, existing only so he could work out his frustrations. I felt less and less like his son. Hell, I began to feel less and less like a human being.

I am the oldest of four, three boys and one girl. My siblings, especially my sister, never received the same beatings I did, and I remember wondering why. For some reason, I also received my sister's punishments. I tried to rationalize this and told myself it had to be because she is a girl and he didn't want to hurt her. Yeah, that had to be it. I tried to drum up any explanation that might help get me through each day. Here I was, still just a kid yet carrying the weight of endless beatings on my shoulders. My self-esteem and my body were taking a serious hit.

Most of the time, I felt as though I was living in the twilight zone. Because of my father's drinking and anger, I never knew which of his behaviors I would get from one day to the next. I learned to hate him and developed a lot of resentment towards my mother as well. Because his violence and anger had been going on for so long, she had somehow gotten used to it and just allowed it. I often wondered why my mother didn't leave him after all the horrible things he did to us. I asked myself often what kind of spell my father had on my mother for her to endure such abuse. He was like some sort of poison or virus that required an antidote. No one knew that I often contemplated killing him. I truly believed that it's only by GOD's grace that I didn't kill my father, considering I would have lengthy conversations with myself about doing it.

Hell, I remember one time my father beat my mother so badly that she finally got the courage to call the cops. When the cops arrived, they arrested him, and my Aunt picked us all up and took us to her house for the night. It was crazy. At the time, we were living on Sawyer Street and when the cops showed up at the house it was in ruins because my father had been beating my mother throughout the house.

My mother's face looked like she had just gone ten rounds with Mike Tyson. On top of all the swelling and blood she was crying. Just looking at her crushed me. My heart hurt for my mother daily. I was the oldest of the children but not yet old enough nor big enough to stand up to my father. I hated to see her go through this, but it happened so often that I sometimes wondered whether she truly wanted it to stop. Every time a court date rolled around she never showed up, so they eventually let him out and the cycle began again.

My father had us living in so much fear of him that when my sister, cousin and I went back into the house after his arrest that day, we ran through in fear gathering up our things as if he was still there. We knew he was gone but his violent presence was so strong throughout the place that we felt as though he was gonna appear at any moment.

As the years progressed we were hoping and praying that things would change and that was one way of getting through those days of war in my home. I often wondered if, in the back of my mother's mind, she was hoping that she could get him to change his abusive behavior.

Chapter Eleven

IN BUSINESS

We eventually moved from Sawyer Street to the Doran Projects when I was about 11 years old. I wished we didn't have to move because I loved living on Sawyer. That's where all my friends were, and I hated the thought of building new friendships all over again.

Being that I was the new guy on the block at Doran, I got into quite a few disputes and fist fights. I believed no one liked me because every time I tried to start a friendship it didn't go well. I was just different, and they did not know how to take me. I think they were all trying to feel me out and I guess that may have been the reason for the fights. Ironically, now that I think back on those days, the very ones I fought ended up being some of my closest associates.

When I lived in the Doran Projects, right before I moved in with my friend JB, I began to dabble into selling weed. Drugs were prevalent there and I knew of a lot of people who smoked it. I started with weed because it was easy to get rid of. I sold nickel bags to my friends, people I knew in my neighborhood as well as those at work. I had to hide it from my parents cause if they knew what I was doing they would have *killed* me, so to speak.

At the time, I felt I had no choice because my income from the restaurant simply was not enough to feed me and my siblings, let alone give my brothers bus fare and lunch money every day, catch the bus to and from work, as well as any other necessities required to survive. Life, in general, was tough for kids growing up in the projects, particularly in our household.

When I was just 16 years old I was introduced to the art of selling crack cocaine, which is powder cocaine cooked into a hard rock-like substance. When I realized how easy it was to get rid of it and how much money I could make, I jumped right in.

Across the street from us lived a Jamaican family who hung out in and around the neighborhood. Some of the guys I had started hanging out with introduced me to them. I slowly got better acquainted once I realized my friends were buying drugs from them. Eventually, I asked one of my guys to take me along the next time they went to buy cocaine from the Jamaican's. I figured I would try my hand at selling it also.

Ironically, I was nervous that my parents might find out what I was up to, not because of the illegal nature of the activity, but I knew if they found out what I was attempting to do they would try to take it from me for their own use, and I would be out of money and work.

I remember the first time I went to purchase crack cocaine. I was uncertain of the price because I had never asked anyone about the going rate. In my mind, tagging along with my buddies each time they made a purchase was my way of building up the courage to buy some myself. Establishing a relationship with the Jamaican family and allowing them to get used to me being around was the best thing I could do. They eventually told me that the cost of an 8-Ball, which is essentially 3.5 grams of crack, would run me $150. So, I took some of my earnings from selling weed and purchased my first 8-Ball.

Though I was well on my way to running my own business, I still knew very little about the drug game. I asked one of the guys I hung out with to show me what type of bags to put the cocaine in and how to bag it up. I started by selling it to neighborhood folks then branched out a little more thanks to new customers I'd met through my existing ones.

It was during this period that I met a skinny guy named Derek, (everyone called him Deek), who would eventually become one of my best friends. I met him through my sister whom he'd dated briefly. Strange as it may seem, I never thought he and I would ever build a bond stronger than the one he and my sister had. Eventually they split up and the awkwardness of them dating was no longer a factor for me.

One day, Deek asked me about going to the Jamaicans to get some cocaine he could sell. At the time I already had some I was trying to get rid of. He asked me if I would go with him to buy some. Deek said, "Rell, how much is it?" I told him it would cost about $150. He told me he had the money. As it turns out, he had swiped some of it from his mom's purse. I tell ya the things we did to survive the streets is not something I recommend.

He asked me to go over to the Jamaicans' house and walk up to the window where they sold the stuff out of. I told him, "No you go." We went back and forth about this for a little while simply because I was not yet comfortable going to their house. After all, I had only been there once before without my buddies. Then he said, "Fuck it I'll go!" I told him we would go together, and we did. Once inside we realized Deek didn't have quite enough money. In his strong accent, the Jamaican in charge said, "Let 'em go." We hurried out of the house and off to the races we went. No one could've imagined the adventures he and I would share over the next few years.

Somehow, my parents eventually figured out what I was up to, so they constantly asked me to give them stuff. They kept telling me that if I refused they would kick me out of the house. They harassed me for months, so with the harassment and everything else going on, I'd finally had enough and went to live with my friend JB. Life went on and over the next couple of years I continued to work, go to school, and sell drugs. My plan was to somehow survive until I got accepted into the Marines or the Firefighter Program.

During my Junior year in high school, my school counselor signed me up to take the next firefighter's exam. Finally, in my Senior year, the opportunity to take the test presented itself. I'll never forget the day we took the exam. Everyone who had signed up to take it was led to an assigned room, where a proctor was ready to give us the test. I remember this being an extremely busy time of year for me because I had also signed up to take the military entrance exam. I was scheduled to report to an office off campus located on East Main Street. This day is also etched in my mind as I remember being so nervous that I vomited right before the test.

I thought of becoming a Marine because I had family in the Marines and some of my friends from school had already signed up as well. I figured I would take both tests which would give me options and opportunities once I graduated high school. All I wanted to do was put myself in a position where I no longer had to struggle. I desperately wanted to get away from hustling and working menial jobs.

The entire process took a little while as I had to have a physical fitness test and be cleared medically to be accepted into both the military and the Fire Fighter's Academy. The waiting period had me feeling extremely anxious as I was so looking forward to this new life I had envisioned in my head.

Once the results from the firefighter evaluation came in the mail I was so nervous I couldn't even open the letter, so I called and asked my sister to come over and open it for me. When she arrived, she took her time opening the letter and reading the contents, further prolonging my anxiety. Of course, at that point I wanted to kill her. She read the results, and though they indicated I had passed the written exam with flying colors, as well as the physical endurance test, unfortunately, I had not passed the medical assessment due to my uncontrolled asthma. I was being denied.

Obviously, I was very disappointed with this news though I naively held out hope that I would still be accepted into the military. Not only did the military qualification results come in the mail, the recruiter also called me. The results indicated that I passed the written portion of the test and the physical fitness portion, but again, had failed the health assessment due to my asthma. Right then and there I felt as though my life had just stopped. I did not know what to do next because I had placed all my faith in these two options.

I hadn't considered going to college after high school because I figured I would attend a university while I was in the service. Thanks to the GI Bill or the Firefighter Academy reimbursement program, I wouldn't have to worry about a large school bill. Otherwise, I felt school was not in the cards for me as I knew I couldn't afford it. I didn't want to go to school and end up with a large debt looming over my head afterwards.

Here I was, 18 years old and no idea where my life was heading as all my plans had suddenly gone out the door. My disappointment was such that a huge feeling of uncertainty fell over me and I just wanted to say, "To Hell with it!" After all, what's the use of making plans when they don't turn out the way you want them to?

There was no question that I now needed a plan B and felt I had to find something that would allow me to earn cash immediately. In my mind, I was like fuck it I'll just keep right on hustling and make this money the best way I know how. See, in my neighborhood you only did one of three things; you worked a 9 to 5 job, punching a clock daily for whomever would consider granting you employment, you hustled something like drugs, clothing, or other odd items, or you got high, which required a different kind of hustle. Our choices as we understood them were extremely limited.

In those days no one was encouraging me to get an education to improve my odds of getting out of the *Hood* and instead, what was pushed was that of getting some type of job that pays you a check every week. This was a priority for many families just to afford to eat every day, put a roof over your head, keep your lights and heat on, and keep clothes on your back.

The struggle was real in the inner-city projects. No one gave out helpful information or provided us opportunities to improve our circumstances. No one alerted us to high paying positions or explained what it would take to obtain them, and we never got advice on how to start a business. I always felt that I was just as smart as some of the people I saw who were in much better circumstances than me. I believed, that given the right opportunity, I would flourish as well.

Instead, it seemed like there was an invisible foot placed on my neck preventing me from moving much in either direction. No progression in life from my family or those in and around my neighborhood. I would often think to myself that there truly had to be something else out there I was missing. How on earth are others thriving while we are stuck here in these roach infested projects just hoping to catch a break. It was very clear to me that there was a huge disparity between those living in the city and those living in the suburbs. I hated it!

I was still just a young guy with very little life experience. I turned to several people for guidance, but given my environment, did not receive the type of advice a person my age needed. Having little choice, I used to get suggestions from the old heads in my family and even from some of their friends. Not sure why I kept doing this because nothing good ever came from their advice. I kept hoping that maybe one day they would have something sound and valid to offer me besides teaching me how to get myself into more trouble and how to do more dirt in the streets.

All I wanted was some hope that although I was unable to get into the Marines or Firefighter Academy, there were other choices available to me. I laugh now because I realize they didn't have a clue just like I had no clue and I was wasting my time even talking to them.

So, I learned how to sell drugs and dabble in illegal activities instead. I started spending money on unnecessary items, became a slave to designer labels, and commenced to destroy my credit. No one taught me how to save for a rainy day, or how to communicate with others. Instead, I bottled up my feelings, learned to mistreat women, got into mischief illegal and otherwise and lived as though there was no tomorrow.

While reflecting on my past, it brings me back to a time when Deek and myself got into some mischief. Well come to think about it, over the years he and I got into a whole lot of mischief... One day we were hustling as usual and we received a page. This is back when pagers were used as a means of communication between the hustler and the user. One of the fiends we used to serve on a regular basis paged me for a package a bit larger than her normal request. So, we head over to her house to see if this request is for real. When we arrive, she announces she's making the request for a friend of hers, who was in the house with her. She then introduces the guy to us. I recognize him from the neighborhood as someone who is a frequent user. I happen to know however that he usually buys from another hustler.

She left us in the kitchen to talk and we set up a way for him to get what he had requested. He wanted to buy half an ounce of crack cocaine. We agreed to meet on a little alleyway close to the projects. Once we got there, Deek said, "Rell, this is a one-way street with no way out.

53

This doesn't seem right let's go!" I said, "Nah, let's get this bread. I have seen this dude in the hood many times copping and getting his little hustle on, so let's just wait a minute more." As we waited, Deek got more impatient and said, "Let's go!" one more time, but just as the words were coming out of his mouth, and I was about to turn around, the dude the girl had put us onto and, and another Jamaican, whom I'd never seen before, came running out of the house carrying a shot gun. At that moment I thought I was going to shit my pants. They were robbing us for the cocaine. All they said was, "Bumbaclod give it tup." In their Jamaican dialect.

They both had their weapons pointed inside the windows of my car. At that moment all I could do was comply with their demands. The Jamaican that was at my window stuck his hand in and began going through my pockets. He took everything I had. As he was going through my pockets he yelled, "Don't move or I'll shoot your Rasclod." I was frozen in fear that they would either kill one or both of us. Lord knows I didn't want that or even have the guilt of my best friend's death on my hands. How on earth would I ever get that image out my head and secondly how on earth would I be able to explain what had happened to his family.

This turn of events angered me so much because before it happened we were beginning to really make some moves and see a little money. Yeah, this was a major setback we couldn't afford, particularly since we still owed the connect. Deek was so angry at me for not leaving when he had suggested it the first time that he kept asking me the same question over and over, "Why the hell didn't you leave? I knew something wasn't right." I didn't know it then, but it turns out Deek has this gift for seeing things, and an uncanny intuition whereby he can envision things before they happen.

I was sick to my stomach and could think of nothing but revenge. Deek and I devised a plan to look for the guys and avenge what they had done to us. We ran to a spot where we'd stashed a Double Barrel Mossberg Shot gun. We grabbed it and proceeded to ride around the neighborhood looking for the fuckers who'd robbed us. We just knew that they were gonna reappear at some point because that neighborhood was their stomping ground.

It wasn't long before we noticed them amongst a crowd standing on the corner of Plymouth and Columbia at a bar called Shantel's, as if nothing had happened. Deek said, "Rell, drive by slowly and I'll lick off," I was like ok, and circled back around. Once I arrived back at the corner where they were standing I yelled, "SHOOT!" But as I said this I came to a complete stop. Obviously, this was a bad Idea, although my windows were tinted my car was bright white and everyone in the neighborhood knew what my car looked like. This meant that when questioned, anyone near the shooting would easily be able to identify and describe my car.

Once stopped I heard Deek in the back-seat yell, "Why the hell are you stopping? Just go! GO! GO! GO!" I was so pissed all I could see was red and wanted them both to pay for what they had done to us. I wanted them to feel the same pain I was feeling. So, I sped down the street and raced back to our spot. Once we got there, Deek kept asking me the same damn questions:

"Why didn't you just leave? Did you sell to them before? Do you know them like that? What the fuck! You know we owe the connect so what are we gonna do now? We have to figure out a way to get this man back his money."

I was at a loss for words and all I could think of at the time was catching that lick and being able to pay the connect a bit sooner than we had anticipated. We sat there for a minute trying to figure out a way to get up out of this large amount of money we now owed. We decided that Deek would give up his classic 1970 Chevy Chevelle as collateral until we could pay the debt. This hurt not only Deek but myself also. The car was amazing, and we used to talk about taking it to car shows at some point and showing her off to the world. We called her "Janet" because she was as beautiful as Janet Jackson. We arranged for the car to be delivered, though all the while, trying to figure out a way to get the car right back.

About a week had passed when we decided we would talk to the connect about possibly making some runs for him, so we could clear the debt. I guess God's favor was shining upon on us that day because it just so happened that the connect needed a new runner as his had recently been arrested for domestic violence.

We agreed to do his running for 30 days at the end of which we should have cleared the debt and he would return the car. We were smiling to ourselves... IT WORKED! We would get Janet back by doing exactly what we would've been doing in the first place, HUSTLING!

Once we got the OK to do the connect's runs Deek figured a way that we could make extra money off each package we delivered. All I could do was say to myself, how the hell does Deek come up with these things.

After this setback had been rectified, and we were able to settle with the connect Deek somehow believed I had set the whole robbery in motion. Because of this, we were not on good terms for quite some time. He asked me if I had done it and of course I denied it because I had nothing to do with it. I asked him, "Why would I do something like that to you? You are like my brother and we have been hustling together for years. If I set you up I'm setting myself up because we eat together. I have never done anything grimy to you."

It hurt that he thought I would pull something like that on him considering all we had been through in the streets. I always felt he was the only one I could rely on and believed he felt the same way about me. I would never do anything to jeopardize that relationship. When you've been in the streets for as long as we had, suspicion has a way of affecting even the closest of relationships. Sad to say but because of this incident we lost touch for a while and it would be a few years before we would reconnect.

Chapter Twelve

COMMUNITY

I didn't have good role models growing up and had no one to look up to. It seemed that all the male figures around me were never available when I needed guidance or advice. When it came to life goals, relationships or finances, I was left to figure those things out on my own.

We kind of bounced around when I was a child and ended up living in several different places and on several different streets in Rochester. Two of those places vividly stand out for me however; #3 Sawyer Street and #44 Doran Street. I remember these two addresses most because we stayed there the longest, and because both streets were situated in real communities. Here, people got to know each other and because of that, eventually established friendships.

Our neighbors were people who cared about what we were into and how productive we were. They would ask about our day, and if they saw us doing something wrong, they would *check* us then report it to our parents. These were typical neighborhoods of the late '70's and '80's, where folks cared and looked out for each other. Looking back, I appreciate those community experiences and have developed a healthy respect for those I now call *my elders*.

During this time in my life, I made friends with the neighborhood children and there really wasn't a time I didn't have someone to hang out with, yet I still felt very much alone. My problem was that I felt I couldn't relate to many of them. My thoughts were different and what I referred to as fun and interesting others thought of as weird or "White", so to speak. To be quite honest many still call me that now as an adult.

Often friends often called me the "white guy" and because of that I often did things to try and fit in, not because I really wanted to do them. I am an introvert by nature, so I didn't mind my own company, though I must admit I did enjoy doing things with the other kids in the neighborhood such as playing hide-and-seek, touch football, *shoot em up, bust em up*, racing bikes, climbing trees, going on bike rides, and hanging at other kids' houses.

As I think about it now, I believe I kept to myself a lot, so I wouldn't have to pretend I was happy at home when I wasn't. I didn't want to hear people make fun of me for talking or acting "White" or that things were ok when they weren't. There was always so much going on at home and I never felt comfortable talking to anyone about it. I was too embarrassed and ashamed. Many of my days were spent hungry and worrying about whether we would be put out on the street, leaving us without a place to lay our heads. Meanwhile, my mom and I were still being beaten at home. If any of my friends had discovered what was going on inside our house I think I might have died of embarrassment.

In those days, everything that went on inside the home was kept a secret and no one had a clue of the level of violence and dysfunction that was taking place in our house. I can't even count the number of times I wanted to run away. The only thing that stopped me was that in running away I would have to explain what was going on at home and with me to whoever's house I ran to, and I couldn't bring myself to do it. I was ashamed. This was my story in a nutshell, and I did not tell a soul. That way I would never have to explain what I was going through nor what I was feeling.

Chapter Thirteen

NO, NOT MY BRO'S!

Meanwhile, though my siblings were not my responsibility, things had taken a bad turn for my little brothers. As I reflect on this period in my life, it takes me to a time when they were just 14 and 15 years old. My parents were now separated, and the boys had returned home to New York to live with my mother after living with my father for a few years. At the time my mother was not yet completely stable and still running the streets a bit. Consequently, my little brothers were also running the streets because they had very little supervision.

I had to go up to their house almost daily just to make sure they went to school. Every day after work I would swing by my mom's house to make sure they had eaten or that there was at least something at the house for dinner. If there wasn't I would pick them up and go grab a pizza or go to the meat market, so I could grab them enough chicken and ground beef to last for the week. By this time, they were already cooking their own meals.

One day, like any other day, after work I headed over to Mom's to check on the boys. I was surprised to find my mother at home when I arrived. She was visibly shaken, and I could tell she'd been crying. She dropped devastating news on me, "The boys have been arrested for armed robbery and murder." I was like "WHAT! What the hell happened?" She filled me in and told me that apparently, they had robbed the corner store right across the street from their apartment. The same store they went to every day to buy snacks and what not.

According to my mother they had gone to school but had left early after which time the robbery happened. She said the only reason she knew about it was because the cops came to her house with information from a tip. They had been told that my little brothers were the ones who robbed the store and shot the store clerk. The officers came inside the house to look for the weapon and to arrest my brothers. Apparently, my youngest brother is the one who shot the store clerk and brought the gun back to the house and upon searching the place the police retrieved the gun from the ceiling of their room and arrested them on site.

Following a thorough search of my mother's residence the officer told her that had my brother not brought the gun back to the house, they would not have been able to arrest them because there was no other evidence linking them to the crime. There was no working surveillance tape and the only witness had told them they were unsure of who did what, but thought it was my brothers because they saw them leave the store shortly after it had happened.

It took some time for all this to sink in but once it did I just broke down and cried. I was devastated because in many ways, I thought of my little brothers as if they were my children. After all, I had essentially been caring for them since the day they were born. I believe this is the first time I ever cried as an adult and it certainly was the last. I felt if I had hurried up and gotten the boys out of my mother's house and into an environment that seemed a bit better they might have flourished and would not have felt the need to do something illegal.

When I eventually got the chance to visit them I asked them individually why they had committed the crime and why they hadn't even approached me to discuss their plan. Each one, at separate moments told me the following,

"Rell, we were tired of you taking care of us. That's Mom and Dad's job and we always felt like we were a burden to you. Every day you spend your money on us, feeding us as if we are your kids. Holidays you do for us in the same way. We are not your kids we are your brothers. We wanted to take the burden off you for a little while."

I couldn't believe it. I reassured them that I didn't mind because they were my brothers, so it was my duty to make sure they were taken care of and to pick up the slack where my parents fell short.

It took some time for me to really get my mind wrapped around this situation and their fate. They had now become a product of the environment in which they were growing up. Simply put, my strong young brothers had become just another set of young black males relegated to the penal system for years. Or simply put, another statistic.

All this did was have me question life even more. My only real reason for living at the time was now gone and would be for double digit years. My heart ached a long time because of this. I felt a part of me was missing because my brothers and I had been together every day. Now, if I wanted to see them I had to visit them in prison and leave them again once the visit was over. Not the life I envisioned for them at all. Sad turn of events to say the least.

Chapter Fourteen

PERSISTENCE

Soon after high school graduation I picked up some construction work at a drywall company. I got this job because my friend and roommate at the time, JB, worked there. I was relieved and happy because It gave me something to do and gave me the sense that I might be on the right path. I worked there for nine years but couldn't get used to not working all year round.

Every winter I had to apply for unemployment, which meant my income would be half what I was making during the summer months. I tried working other jobs during the winter months, but they were all menial labor-intensive jobs that lead nowhere. I eventually felt I was wasting my time and that this cycle of seasonal work was taking me nowhere fast.

One day I heard the Eastman Kodak Company was conducting open interviews in Rochester, NY so I got my resume together and went down in hopes that I would be hired for an available position.

A month went by and still no response from Kodak. By this time, I needed once again to apply for unemployment as the drywall company's season had ended. Again, knowing the money I would be receiving would not be enough to live on, I applied to a temporary work agency. Ironically, turns out the agency was contracted to hire for Kodak and they offered me a position.

Although it was only a temporary position, I was excited about it as I felt it was a way of getting my foot in the door. I hoped I would be able to prove myself and possibly get hired permanently. So, I went for it and quit my job at the drywall company with hopes that I would never have to return.

By this time, I was about 21 years old and had my first child, a beautiful baby girl. Her birth was an eye-opening experience. Having a little one of my own was a lot of responsibility and I knew it required some stability. I realized more than ever that I needed to find-full time work because I now had another mouth to feed. So, the pressure was on to get myself together for my child's sake at least. Just finding full-time, stable employment was becoming more and more of a challenge.

My job assignment, at Kodak, was for one year with the promise that when the time was up, they would consider hiring me full-time. I worked all year and when it came time for my year-end evaluation my supervisor told me they were on a hiring freeze but that they would consider extending my contract for another year. I know companies do this to save money on wages and health insurance. I must admit, I was disappointed but It sure beat working for the drywall company, plus the job was pretty easy.

I was a forklift operator and worked in the warehouse delivering film and supplies to the assembly line workers. I loaded and unloaded trailers and never really had to get off the forklift. I loved it because it didn't require the intense labor my previous position had. This went on for another year but by this time Kodak was undergoing huge layoffs, and of course, being that I was a temp worker I got cut first.

I was really disappointed because I felt I couldn't catch a break. With this unexpected turn of events, I went over to the drywall company and successfully talked my way into getting my old job back. Shortly after I returned to work there however, I noticed how bad my health was becoming. I now remembered this was another reason I had wanted to find something else.

I worked for them for an additional year and a half but was eventually taken out of work by my doctor. This all happened in 1999 and I'll never forget it. I was hospitalized for a severe asthma attack which put me in the hospital for 10 days. While in hospital a social worker came to my room to tell me that my doctor recommended I sign up for Social Security Disability. The doctor had informed her of the deterioration in my lungs resulting from the effects of inhaling drywall dust every day for several years. Here I was, just 27 years old and they were trying to put me on disability!

The social worker initiated the application process and after months and months of waiting, doctor's appointments, social security hearings, and physicals, I finally got approved. Though in some ways this was good news, I was once again at a crossroads because the amount of money I'd been approved for would in no way be enough for me to live on. On the one hand I had been awarded a consistent income source but on the other, I was not allowed to make money above the SSD cap, which essentially put me between a rock and a hard place. Additionally, since I would be receiving SSD, my daughter would also receive a stipend from them. This was the only other benefit from this turn of events which meant I would be able to provide for my daughter's needs, which had been a huge concern of mine. Although it wasn't a tremendous amount it would be something.

Consequently, I figured I had no choice but to get back into the game. I didn't want to, and I wondered how and why I had ended up in this situation again, and how on earth I was ever going to get out. Life has not been a friend to me and nothing ever went smoothly. I knew there had to be a better way, but I just couldn't see my way through it at the time.

Chapter Fifteen

BACK IN THE GAME

Hence, another chapter had begun in my life, this time it involved me getting back into the game. I chose this lifestyle out of necessity. I had very few choices and a family to provide for. No positions paying a living wage were hiring felons and my health prevented me from obtaining any construction work.

It took me some time and effort to get back into the swing of things. I knew I did not want to be hanging out on street corners again, and I knew I absolutely did not want anything to do with selling crack ever again.

Crack cocaine is one of the forms of cocaine, which is produced from powder cocaine and is smoked. Crack is essentially powder cocaine mixed with water and baking soda which is dried into a solid mass. This mass is 'cracked' into rocks that are smoked.

By this time, not only was crack cocaine known to be more psychologically addicting than powdered cocaine, it also was accompanied by the most drama and the legal penalties were extremely high. Because of the highly addictive quality of crack cocaine, the government had instituted several laws to try and eliminate the possession and sale of it. It was a dangerous game to get into.

Also, seeing what crack had done to my parents and others in my neighborhood, made me not want to

70

have anything to do with it anymore. Plus, the other problems that came along with hustling crack like getting robbed by the fiends, stick up kids and other dealers, and being up all hours of the night answering the phone. There were also scores of addicted women, who would offer sex in exchange for crack and there were fiends that tried to sell me jewelry (whether real or fake), food stamps, tv's, guns (whether they worked or not), bikes, clothes, and a whole host of other random stuff. Although crack was extremely profitable, I definitely no longer wanted any part of selling it. It just seemed to bring too many problems with it and I began to see it as a cancer that destroys everyone and everything in its path.

I soon realized that powder cocaine and marijuana were the two items in highest demand, so that's what I went with. I went around talking to people who were hustling on the block, those involved in the night life, and to people I needed to line up in order to make a true go of this. It took some doing to reestablish myself, but after a month or two I had connected with enough people willing to buy from me. I was then able to purchase my own package and start making money.

Powder cocaine sales are much easier to manage than dealing in crack. In my experience the powder cocaine customer is more typically from a rural or suburban environment, uses the drug for social events and parties, and is not as feverishly addicted to the drug. To get going, I started out very light. A friend of mine fronted me a quarter pound of weed and I also purchased a quarter ounce of powder cocaine. Another acquaintance brought me into a circle of people who snorted lines and partied every weekend. He had a system whereby he would go to a couple of nightclubs each night and customers would simply be there waiting for him. There was nothing to it and it seemed very easy to do.

It was during this time that I reconnected with my old friend Deek. Deek and my sister happened to run into each other one day at a club he owned and exchanged information. Funny thing was, the way he and I connected the first time we met was the same way we reconnected, which was through my sister.

I couldn't help but think that the universe has a way of bringing life around full circle. At the time I didn't think that we would ever have a chance at rebuilding our relationship to what it once was, heck I honestly at one time I thought I would never see Deek again. They say God brings people into your life for a reason, a season or a life-time. I was beginning to think Deek was one of those people who would remain in my life forever.

I was happy that we were able to settle that old issue that had been looming over my head for so many years. Being able to talk and clear the air was the best feeling in the world and after we did this it was just like we had never lost touch in the first place. I got my best friend back and it was time to see what kind of moves we could make together.

So, once I learned the ropes on this side of the fence got my weight up and made a little money. I attempted to pull my buddy Deek into the circle and teach him what I had learned about this new process.

I would go by his house quite a bit because he kept a little after-hours spot in the back that we called the BOOM-BOOM ROOM. We had so much fun there partying, laughing, drinking, listening to music, and socializing. It eventually became my go-to place of escape after a long day of hustling.

By this time, Deek was removing himself from the game all together and focusing on his new marriage and young family and instead he started getting into real-estate. Come to think about it, I would have to be the reason he got back in the game. We teamed up again, after we had lost touch for a while, and began to make money together. Just like old times. After some time however, Deek got into his own groove and created his own lane with his own people. He started doing things on a much grander scale which allowed us to keep even more of our earnings in house. Until that moment I forgot how well we worked together. If I was out of work and he had work left I would help him out and vice versa. Life was pretty good during that time because we were doing reasonably well financially.

This whole strategy was starkly different from selling bags of crack on the corner of Frost and Jefferson Avenue or hustling out of some crack fiend's house on

Thurston Road. I was like, hey I can hang out, have fun, and make money in the process...why not? In addition to hanging out at the clubs every weekend, on Thursdays, I bagged up $500 worth of cocaine and traveled 40 miles outside the city, where customers stood in anticipation of my arrival. I'd sell out within minutes every single time! I suggested Deek come along but he immediately said, "Hell no, I am not fucking with that little ass town and I suggest you don't either. Boy, I don't need those kinds of problems and neither do you."

Like all small towns it was a gold mine. Whatever the value of a bag in the city the same bag would cost double there. So, at the end of my visit I would bring home $1,000 or more unless someone came up short. I didn't really care if they did because, in the grand scheme of things, I was making much more than the coke's actual street value anyway. After doing this for a while customers began to ask me if I could get them some weed and as they put it, if I could get my hands on some a that ooooo weeee, which is a term we use for the really good stuff. Unfortunately, as stated in the bible, "Ill-gotten gains do not profit, but righteousness delivers from death."

-Proverbs 10:2

One day where I had planned on driving to the town, it started out like a typical day except that my wife and I had gotten into a big fight right before I was scheduled to leave. Because of this I did things slightly differently than I normally would. I decided to pick up my cousin, so I'd have someone to drive me there because I was so angry that I wanted to drink, and smoke weed the entire way there, which is exactly what I did.

I picked up my cousin, stopped at the store, and bought a six-pack of beer and some blunts to roll my weed in then we hit the road. I rolled up the weed and popped open a Red Stripe because at the time, that was my beer of choice. I fired up the blunt, took a few hits, and passed it to my cousin for him to hit it too. As he puffed away, I began to spill my guts about the argument my wife and I had before I left. I just felt I needed to vent. So, I go on and on explaining to him what had happened and before I knew it we had almost reached the town exit. Just as we were entering the town an officer appeared behind us with his lights flashing. We were being pulled over...

Chapter Sixteen

SHIT JUST GOT REAL

We were so into our conversation that I didn't realize what was going on until my cousin said very loudly, "OH SHIT THE COPS!" I immediately went into *what the heck we should do* mode. The car smelled like weed which I knew was probable cause to search it without a warrant. We had open containers of alcohol in the car as well. Two definite no-noes'. My cousin slowly pulled the car over and while he's doing that I rolled down my window to let the smoke out of the car, so it didn't smack the officer dead in the face when my cousin rolled down his window.

As the officer walked towards the car, my mind was racing as I wondered how the hell we were going to get out of this one unscathed. The officer began to ask my cousin the following questions:
"Do you know why I am pulling you over?" To which my cousin says "No." Then the officer says, "I'm pulling you over for view obstruction. Did you know that your windshield boarder on the car can be no wider that six inches?" I then interjected by saying, "No officer I did not, but I don't believe it is bigger than six inches." The officer continued and said, "Well I have to measure it to make sure." But as he's talking and scanning the inside of the car, I realize that he has spotted the open container. He says, "I see you've been drinking. How much have you had? Do you know it's illegal to have an open container in

your vehicle?" He pauses for a moment then continues, "I also smell marijuana coming from inside the car. I am going to have to ask you to step out of the vehicle." While he's telling my cousin this I interject by saying, "The weed is mine and so is the bottle of beer. I asked my cousin to drive because I knew I was going to be drinking." The officer then asked my cousin for his license and unbeknownst to me, his license had been suspended for a previous DWI. Something he hadn't told me, though I must admit, I had never asked.

As the officers pull us out of the vehicle I continue rambling on about the alcohol being mine and that it did not belong to my cousin. I didn't want him getting into trouble for something I'd chosen to do. I also told the officers that the weed was mine. As I'm telling them this, one of the officers asks me where the weed is? I then hand them the small bag of weed I had in my pocket from which I had rolled the blunt we were smoking, along with the half-smoked blunt. I did this in hopes that it would pacify them and therefore they would not search my car.

Now, as I'm sizing up the officers I can tell that one of them is a veteran cop, whereas the other one looks fresh out of the academy. He was very young probably only in his mid-twenties. The older officer had us standing outside by the front of the car while the younger one went to his car to call in the stop and do whatever it is they do when they call in your license, insurance, and registration.

The older officer orders us to stand where we are and tells us he is going to search the car. At this point my heart started beating rather quickly and I felt like my stomach was going to explode. I was certain I was going to hurl all over the place. All I could do was hope that he'd overlook everything I had stashed in the car.

He eventually stopped searching and came out of the car with nothing. I felt a huge sigh of relief though unfortunately that turned out to be short-lived. Once the younger officer had finished checking our license information he decided he too wanted a go at searching the vehicle. A few minutes later I heard him proclaim, "Jackpot! Look what we have here." He pulled out what he'd found in my car and started setting it out on the hood. At that moment all I could do was shake my head and say to myself, "Welp you know what time it is." I instantly went into bail out mode saying to myself "Ok Terrell how much money you got in stash for bail, who still owes you money that you can access quickly and who can you call to get things in motion?"

I knew at that moment that I was going to jail and there was nothing I could do to stop it. After he'd finished searching and tearing up my car I heard them talking. The younger officer asked the older one, "I thought you searched the car?" The older officer replied, "I did I guess I just didn't check the container of cookies he had." What I had done was hide the drugs amongst the chocolate chip cookies I had purchased just in case something like this happened. My hope was that they would feel the cookies and leave the bag alone, which is essentially what the older officer had done. The other officer just happened to look inside the bag and saw what I had stashed there.

Everything inside the car had been discovered and was spread all over the hood of my car. A news team suddenly showed up on the scene and was taking pictures of all the evidence. What they ended up retrieving was an 62 grams of cocaine all bagged up and ready for resale and a quarter pound of weed. In terms of cash all they found was about $50 in singles which they fanned out on the car to make it look like there were hundreds of dollars seized. Also, they retrieved a pair of brass knuckles and a taser.

They finally got around to cuffing us and seating us in separate vehicles. The officer who detained me began to read me my rights and after doing so, the very first question he asked was if I wanted to cooperate with law enforcement. I had the biggest blank stare on my face and you would have thought I'd seen a ghost. I asked the officer to repeat himself just to make sure I'd heard him correctly. He repeated his question to which I immediately responded with, "HELL NO!" This pissed the officer off and he began to curse me out and call me all kinds of names. As this is going on I start laughing which angers the officer more. He yells, "Shut the fuck up before I make you!" I responded by saying, "Um no, I'm not talking and when did it become illegal to laugh." I continued to laugh a little while longer simply because I knew I was getting under his skin.

He then drove me to the police station. On the way he asked more questions but by now, I'm totally ignoring him. Upon arrival at the station, the officer takes me out of the car and into the police barracks then sticks me into a room and handcuffs me to a table which is cemented to the floor. What appears to be two detectives came into the room and began interrogating me. I immediately requested lawyer and my phone call. I said to them, "I really don't know why you chose to stick me in this room. What I need is to get in touch with my lawyer." They said to me, "Do you realize how much trouble you're in? You were trafficking over county lines." I said, "Whatever! I have nothing else to say!" I wanted to see if they were going to violate my rights. If they had I would then have something to use against them, but unfortunately that did not happen.

They processed me then stuck me in a cell with all the others that had been arrested that day. I spotted my cousin sitting across the way which lessened my fear that he might disclose something to the cops. All I could do at that point was sit and stew in the uncertainty of the case. I was very much aware that small towns usually give out stiffer penalties than large cities do.

Chapter Seventeen

THEY GOT ME

When they led me to court for my arraignment hearing they slapped both of us with a ridiculously high bail. My cousin was getting more and more upset that he was sitting in a cell next to me especially since he had nothing to do with the drugs that were found in the car. I had to remind him on several occasions that I had made it clear that the contraband was mine and that I was taking responsibility for the drugs.

Unbeknownst to me however, the only reason they were holding my cousin was for driving without a license. They weren't even charging him with drug possession. They were trying to pin a *Driving While Under the Influence* charge on him. I didn't find any of this out until my lawyer had been secured and I was finally out on bail. I felt relieved that they weren't charging him with possession because It had never been my intent for him to get into trouble because of what I had going on.

Going through the court process for this charge had me extremely stressed out simply because of the way the system tends to work in smaller towns. It is my opinion that they try and make an example of anyone caught up in the justice system. Crimes like these are big news until the moment of sentencing. I had an idea of how it might go but nothing was certain. My lawyer told me he worked out a deal with the DA, but it would be up to the judge to go along with it. The day came for my sentencing and they charged me with Criminal Possession of a Controlled Substance in the 3rd degree, felony, Unlawful Possession of Marijuana 5th degree, misdemeanor, Criminal Possession of a Weapon 4th degree, felony.

My lawyer tried to work out sending me to a program that would either allow me to be home within a year or go to Shock Camp which would have me home within six months. When these options were presented before the Judge he stated that I did not qualify for either program because I now had a violent felony attached to my charges because of the weapons. First, I had no clue that just possessing those two items was a crime and secondly, I had no idea it was considered a violent crime considering neither had been used. I thought it was safe to buy them because they sell them as novelty items in Spencer's and therefore it wasn't an illegal pistol. Boy was I wrong!

Now because the judge didn't accept the program deal my lawyer asked for a continuance to which the Judge responded with a resounding, "NO! This case was set for sentencing today and I'm going to sentence your client today! You may have a 30-minute recess to speak with your client but prepare for sentencing when you come back in front of me."

My lawyer and I went out of the courtroom to talk. He told me my only other option was to settle for a sentence of two to four years with a Shock Camp recommendation, which would have me home within six months but spending the rest of my sentence on parole. I agreed because it seemed like the only other sensible option I had.

We go back before the Judge and the DA indicates that his recommendation was a two to four-year sentence with the recommendation of Shock Camp and Shock Parole upon completion of the program. My lawyer asked me was I ok with this and I said yes because I thought I would be home in a few months anyway. Boy was I in for a surprise!

I was taken into custody immediately following sentencing. I was hoping to get a furlough, so I could stay out a little while longer then turn myself in at a later date, but the Judge was not trying to hear that. The Judge was a hard nose and didn't go for any nonsense. After sentencing, my lawyer came up with the idea that I could potentially get my sentence reduced but it would require that the weapons charge be reduced to a misdemeanor or thrown out altogether. If this happened my sentence would change drastically.

A week later I received a letter from my lawyer with the results from the court. The court denied my lawyer's attempt at reducing or vacating one of my charges. This upset me because I so was hoping and praying this could work. Since it didn't I just began to prepare myself to go through the Shock Camp Program.

A month after that I heard one of the deputies calling my name. He said, "Brady pack up, you're on this morning's transport upstate." This made me extremely nervous because I'd heard so many horror stories from guys who'd been upstate about the things they had endured. Plus, I'd watched several movies over the years which were now flooding my thoughts about what I would face in the prison system.

The deputies proceeded to handcuff me and shackle my feet together, which made it hard to walk. They then shackled me to another prisoner. I had heard that they do that, but I wasn't sure if it was true or not. Unfortunately, it was as true as the rumors about the disgusting food we were served daily. Before shoving everyone on the bus for transport they placed a metal lock box on our handcuffs which restricted our hand and wrist movement even more. The box covered the chain that separates the cuffs and the lock completely. If anyone had a plan to get out of the cuffs, their desire was further complicated by the box.

Once we were all cuffed and shackled to one another they began to shove us up onto the bus two at a time. The seats were very uncomfortable and there were bars on the windows. The windows were also tinted so passers-by couldn't see who was on the bus. I'm sure many figured out it was a bus full of prisoners nonetheless seeing that the side of the bus read: Orleans County Correctional Facility.

We finally arrive at the Elmira Correctional Facility which is considered a reception facility. This is where most prisoners go to become classified and then to be transported to whichever prison has room and fits their classification. Upon arrival, the first thing they make you do is to strip down naked to check you for contraband. They have you lift your feet, so they can look at the bottom of them and they make you wiggle your toes. They force you to lift your genitals, open your mouth, stick out your tongue, then bend over and spread your butt cheeks so they can look inside your butt to see if you might be trying to smuggle something into the prison.

Once all the cavity checks are complete, they make you shave the hair off your head and face, then they apply a white powder on you to kill any lice. They don't apply the powder gently either, instead they throw it on you as if you're some disgusting germ they want to exterminate.

I've never felt more naked in my life. There I was standing naked as a jay bird feeling as though my life had officially ended. Humiliated I finally received my uniform and boots to put on. The state provides two uniforms, one pair of state boots, a pair of state sneakers, which looked like generic Converses, six pairs of white boxers, six white t-shirts and six pairs of white socks. This was standard across the board for every inmate entering the system of corrections.

It's demeaning and enduring this process multiple times is taxing on the psyche. I know this must be a tactic designed to humble those entering the prison system, to remind us of who is boss, and to tear down aggressive, tough guy attitudes.

Following this humiliating experience, the deputies took all the new guys and assigned them an inmate DIN number and an ID card which I'll never forget. My DIN# was 03 B 2142. A DIN is assigned to each inmate admitted to the Department of Corrections and Community Supervision. It's an internal number used to identify each inmate. The DIN has three parts; a 2-digit number, a letter, and a 4-digit number. They come up with the two-digit number based on the year you were committed to corrections and the last four numbers indicate the order in which you came through reception. The letter is the facility identifier. In my case the "B" stood for the Elmira Correctional Facility which is where I went through the reception process.

Once the deputies have finished processing you, not only do you get your assigned clothing, but you also get a bed roll which consists of a blanket, two sheets, two rags, a towel, a small bar of soap, a tooth brush, a mini tube of tooth paste and a bucket or some type of plastic pail.

Once everyone has received their stuff the deputy makes everyone line up in single file then walks you through the gallery. The gallery is the ground floor of reception where a sizable number of inmates watch as you walk by. The inmates in cells on either side of you are

86

yelling, talking loudly, and doing whatever else they do. Once you begin the walk the other inmates yell things at you and if someone recognizes you they acknowledge you and generally shout something along the lines, "If you need something I got you, or I'll fly you a kite." A kite is a note of some sort.

After all this I finally made it to my cell and by this time it was late, and I was hungry. We hadn't eaten, and dinner time was over. They eventually came around and gave us each two bologna sandwiches wrapped in plastic wrap, mustard packets, and two cookies. I was so hungry that I ate both sandwiches like they were rare slices of prime rib au jus, mashed potatoes, and asparagus. I just sat back and imagined the cookies were Cheesecake Factory made. I fantasized that I was out late having a meal I deserved because I had completed some major item on my task list. I tell you, the imagination is a very useful and powerful tool when in a place like that. And trust me I used my imagination quite often while there.

Now the fun begins... After a couple weeks I was essentially sent to the shock camp facility they'd assigned me to. The moment we arrive an officer jumps on the bus yelling at the top of his lungs like the bus was on fire. It reminded me of something I'd seen on T.V. They had everyone run off the bus and line up as though we were in the military. The officers went down the line of guys and would get into your face talking at the top of their lungs cursing, calling you names and trying to get a rise outta ya.

From the moment we ran off the bus we were made to run everywhere. With me having asthma as bad as I do I simply couldn't do it. A couple days of running and I was sent to the infirmary for two days due to a severe asthma attack. I tried telling them over and over that there was no way I could do all that running and non-stop physical activity required but they didn't believe me, and they were not trying to hear it, until I almost collapsed.

At this point I was considered medically unable to complete the program and placed back on the draft to be transported to a medium classified prison facility. This change meant I would be completing my entire prison sentence because I was no longer eligible for the program that would have reduced my sentence. Boy did this suck because I had been looking forward to being home in a few months verses a couple years. Something else my health prevented me from being able to take advantage of.

Chapter Eighteen

SPIRITUAL ROOTS

As children we went to church faithfully every Sunday for years until my parents began partying on the regular. Growing up in the church and learning about God and his promises caused me to question the turmoil I was going through at home. Was God punishing me for something? I wondered whether I deserved to live a good life or not? Was I destined to be punished by those who were supposed to love me? These questions burdened me for years as my nightmare of a life continued.

My relationship with the church didn't end after my parents stopped going. I continued to go on my own and walked to church by myself every Sunday for years. I kept going because I felt there was something more I needed to know about God and how he might help make my life better. There had to be something I was missing and there had to be some justification for me growing up in a living hell!

I would often look to the heavens, throw up my hands, shake my head and wonder where God was. On many occasions I questioned God, "God aren't you supposed to be my protector? I thought as my Heavenly Father you are supposed to be my savior? Why are you not punishing those that are persecuting me? How long will you allow these things to go on in my life? Father God do you really exist? There were so many times I felt like an empty shell and when I was most discouraged, I often asked these questions of God.

Just as I felt I couldn't take it any longer and felt that God had left my side, He would offer a sense of relief in my life. Something would happen that would cause me to admit that it had to be due to godly intervention. I remember a day when I received one of my usual ass whoopings, but this time it was a bit more intense. In addition, on that same day, my father had jumped on my mom. Then later that night he went out drinking. Hours had passed, and he hadn't made it home. Around two in the morning my mom received a call from the state police that my father had gotten into an extremely bad car accident in which he had broken his neck and had to be rushed to the hospital. Although this was a terrible thing that happened, it relieved my mother and myself of many weeks of abuse at the hands of my father as it took that long for him to heal from his injuries.

Eventually, my sister met a guy who was a couple years older than she was. He was 18 and she was 16 when they started dating. They met when she moved away from home and began living with one of her friends. My sister never uttered a word to anyone at home that she was dating an older guy. Within just a few months she was pregnant. Although my sister became pregnant she sought to complete high school through a program for pregnant teens called The Young Mother's Program.

My sister gave birth to a baby boy and when he turned five years old I started to take him everywhere with me. I felt the need to expose him to a life with God and was determined to protect him from experiencing the same abuse I had. I truly loved my nephew and spent a lot of time with him. I felt it was my God-given duty to teach him things I hadn't learned while growing up, including how to be Christlike and live a God-fearing life.

When I arrived at the prison, I immediately signed up for church services. I figured I owed God my full attention while I was incarcerated, considering I hadn't given him any of my time while I was running the streets. Obviously, I had a lot of time to think and I slowly realized I had begun to worship money which is something one should never do. As the good book indicates in I Timothy 6:10, "For the Love of Money is the root of all evil." I saw myself chasing after it and taking all kinds of unnecessary risks to obtain it. Not good at all. I stopped listening to those who tried to warn me about how reckless I had become. Though I knew some of the decisions I made weren't such good ideas, I just kept doing that shit anyway.

I didn't care about much and I now know this was reflected in my behavior. I stopped giving back and my time was spent in bars and clubs and never in church. Instead, I should've been giving thanks for all that I had and the ability to enjoy it because GOD had blessed me with another day of life. I don't know what changed in me because this was not like me at all. My behavior was inconsistent with who I am and how I let my recklessness consume me is beyond me. I knew better. Anytime God was at the forefront of my life things have gone much smoother. Of course, I had trials and tribulations, but I had God's promises and strength to hold onto to help get me through.

They say when the devil grabs a hold of you it sometimes takes a while to shake him loose. God may bring you to your knees, so you can recognize just who HE is and the power HE possesses. Gravitating to any one thing and being obsessed with it to the point where it consumes your life becomes idolization or worshiping of that thing. I had forgotten these principals which I had held true for so much of my life. It was time to get back to my roots and giving God his due praise.

So, during my stay I got involved in church services and stayed active through my release. Doing this helped me stay focused on something positive and not dwell on my circumstances. I knew God was trying to tell me something and I needed to sit still long enough to hear what it was. I didn't realize this fact for the first year I was inside because I was more focused on getting out than sitting still and listening or allowing God to work on me. There were opportunities for early release which were all denied for one reason or another and I believe now that it was a door God kept closed because I still hadn't gotten the message he needed me to get. Once it was time I knew

God would release the locks on the doors and allow me another chance at this here thing called life.

I met some good brothers who gave their testimonies on how God delivered them from the grip of the devil and that old life, and how their life had changed for the better because of the decisions they'd made. We are all given choices and as one brother put it, you can opt to use your choice for bad or for good. He said we all fall short of the Glory of God but never let it bring you down so far that you can't bring it back up. Another brother told me that we all have gifts God has bestowed upon us whether we want to believe it or not. He said you were not placed on this earth for any purpose other than bringing good into someone's life.

We all meet for a reason and serve an equally important purpose in one another's lives. Whether it's to give a word, lend a helping hand, or to educate, just try not to ever let the lesson pass you by. Always be open to receiving a blessing as well as being a blessing. You never know whose life you're affecting or who is affecting your life.

After listening to the brother's testimony, I felt that my life had no balance at all. I needed God in my life regardless of the things I was doing. This way HE could guide me through the good and the bad things. Gaining strength, wisdom, and guidance from the almighty God is the only way to live. Recognizing this fact took me some time but once I did the day to day seemed to get much easier.

It's strange how quickly we forget how well we lived once we became spiritually connected in comparison to when we weren't. A hard lesson I had to learn more than once... Not fun! They say the meaning of insanity is doing the same thing over, and over again, yet expecting a different result. Well that was me in a nutshell. Always forgetting about God and placing everything and everyone in front of him. If there's any one piece of advice I can give people in general, it's to NEVER forsake the creator and always make him a part of your life. Bringing perfect balance to life requires a spiritual component.

Chapter Nineteen

PEOPLE CAN CHANGE

Speaking of the power of God, I witnessed firsthand a miraculous transformation that only HE could've maneuvered. Considering all the damage my father had done in my lifetime, there came a point where I wondered if he would ever get himself together. I also questioned whether he and I would ever be able to repair our relationship. I was well aware that some people get to a place where they just can't come back from drugs and alcohol. I've witnessed how that life can grab hold of you and never let you go.

Watching from the sidelines as my parents lives unraveled, I used to pray and ask God to release them from the demons that were encapsulating them. I wanted so deeply to have my parents back and not just for my sake, but especially for my siblings. Because I was the oldest I felt it was too late for me, but it wasn't too late for my little brothers.

My father attempted rehab a few times. He would come home and do good for a while then go right back to his old habits, hanging out with the same people and at the same places. This was always the determining factor to me whether he was going to be successful or not. Come to think about it, it took my father four tries at rehabilitation followed by a move to another state for him to get himself together and stay clean.

95

Once he finally got clean for good, we slowly began to build our relationship. I had gotten to a point in my life where I no longer cared whether it happened or not. I was also hurting even more for my little brothers because if anything they needed him more now than they needed me.

My father felt the only way he was going to kick drugs was to move away from the people and places that perpetuated his addiction. So, he moved to Pittsburgh, PA, as he had family that lived there so at least he would have some support. The only thing keeping him in Rochester at this point was his marriage to my mom and us kids. So, he and Mom discussed the move. She did not want to relocate so after much debate they decided to divorce instead. They agreed my father would take my little brothers with him for a few years and raise them by himself. And that's exactly what he did. My mother was very upset and became quite bitter when all this was going on because she blamed my father for the situation she was in. She also felt he was the reason she'd begun using in the first place.

I was optimistic for my father however, because he finally did something to better himself. During his time in Pennsylvania he realized he wanted and needed to build a relationship with God and got to know him more intimately. He eventually attended seminary to become a minister. He completed his schooling and went from ministering in the congregation to pastoring his own church! Talk about redemption.

I was extremely proud of him and was ecstatic to witness his transformation. He still used corporal punishment on my little brothers, but he was no longer an alcoholic or drug addict. I saw this as God continuing to work on him. After all, he had been one way for years and years and it would take some time to completely transform into a man of God.

To see the changes in him and to have civilized conversations with him had me in utter amazement for a long period of time. It was like I couldn't believe it. We had never had conversations when I was growing up. And, as our relationship continued to grow, I no longer felt as I once had towards him and any thoughts of wanting him dead and out my life eventually left me.

My father's transformation and our continued communication and relationship building strengthened while I was in prison the first time. During my time there I talked to him about life, our relationship, and my own family, which now included a wife and children. Amazingly, as dysfunctional as his own marriage had been, he was actually able to provide me with insight on mine. He even gave me sound advice on raising my children. Ironic, right?

I couldn't figure out how he could provide me with valuable information, so I asked him about it. He simply replied; "Terry, all I can say is I grew up. It took me a while, but I did. I was able to get advice from your grandfather, who turned out to be one wise man. Now, I'm giving it to you." He also said, "I'm sorry I wasn't there for you like I should have been through the years and I apologize for the load you had to take on with your sister and brothers. Because of that however, you've become a great man and I see how much of a caretaker you are to everyone around you. You are a good man Terry. I just wish you hadn't needed to spend this time in jail. I wish it hadn't happened to you. But I will tell you this, make this time count. Pray and read your bible and rebuild your relationship with God."

While building a relationship and communicating weekly, Dad informed me of just how bad he was doing medically. For some reason he sensed that he didn't have much time left to live. We discussed him moving in with me and my family once I returned home from prison. This way I would be able to keep an eye on him and get him to his doctor's appointments etc. We talked about this more seriously once I had received my release papers.

Two weeks prior to my release date my father asked me, "Terry when will you be home I'm trying to wait on you." The way he said it was as if he knew he was going to die and he was trying to hold on until I returned home. I said, "Dad I'll be home in two weeks please hold on I'm coming." He said, "I will try." That really bothered me for the next couple of days. We talked again once more and then two days later I received notice from the prison chaplain to come down to his office. I found this strange considering I'd only just seen him at church service on Sunday and again at bible study on Wednesday night. This was only Tuesday, so why was he requesting my presence? I knew something was up...

When I arrived at his office, the first thing he said to me was, "Hello son, your sister called and needs you to call home as soon as possible." I asked him what for and he told me, "Just make the call. I'll give you some privacy." I called my sister and when she picked up the phone I could hear her crying on the other end of the line. I asked her what was wrong, and her response was, "Dad is dead! He died today. He went to dialysis, fell asleep and never woke up." I literally froze. I couldn't find any words, and I was literally stuck. All I could get out was, "No way, you kiddin, right?" I just talked to him two days ago. We had discussed him coming to live with me upon my release in two weeks. How on earth could this happen? He hadn't seemed that bad off when I spoke with him. Certainly not sick enough to be dead right now." My sister just continued crying and after I finished talking she started yelling at the top of her lungs saying, "HE'S DEAD TERRELL, HE'S FUCKING DEAD! I WOULDN'T MAKE THIS SHIT UP!" So, I just told her to please calm down and relax. I knew she wouldn't make it up, but this was just my initial reaction and way of dealing with the news. I simply couldn't believe it. Over and over in my head I kept replaying our recent conversation, which had only taken place TWO DAYS before this unexpected and tragic news.

After my father's death, I began to feel a measure of guilt. I felt that, had I not put myself in a position that landed me in prison, I could've spent more time with my dad. I would have seen to it that once he transitioned he received the funeral he had hoped for. My sister was in no shape to cope with his funeral arrangements and wasn't aware of his final wishes because they had never spoken about them. I was the only one in constant contact with him and knew what he wanted and where he wanted to be buried.

It's times like this where I beat myself up for the choices I've made. It was also a realization of how short life can be and just how unpredictable it is. I never wanted to go through anything like this ever again. This experience did something to me spiritually and I prayed I'd never hear of the death of an immediate family member and be unable to attend their service nor have input in the burial itself. To this day I still think about it and feel guilt over it. Deep down I know there was nothing I could have done about the timing, but I also know that had I made different choices I could have been present instead of locked up miles away from my family.

Chapter Twenty

SECOND TIME AROUND

The day I was arrested, the second time for Drug possession, was a day like any other. It was the July 4th weekend, one day after I had dropped my wife off at the airport. She had left on vacation to Jamaica, a trip I should've gone on with her but foolishly opted out of thinking I wouldn't be able to obtain a passport.

The next morning, I got up and started my runs like any other day only this time I had packed my truck with a considerable amount more product. I had five pounds of weed and a few bags of cocaine in my vehicle. My thought was that I would be wise to prepare ahead of time for all the runs I had to make so I wouldn't have to return home and restock. After all, I had preorders, so I knew it would be gone soon and that it was just a matter of time before I had connected with each client.

When evening rolled around, I was still trying to figure out what it was I was going to do since my wife was out of town. I figured I would hang out with some friends and we all decided to meet up at a bar to have some drinks. We then decided to bar hop and see what was going on at several places. We eventually decided to go to a place that used to be called *Double Days*, a local neighborhood bar that serves strong, reasonably priced drinks. By then, it was 1 a.m. and the bar was closing in an hour which meant we would have to rush to get there.

101

We set out by following each other in a convoy, but once we jumped on the expressway some decided to race each other and lost the rest of us in traffic. Once I hit the off-ramp I looked in my rearview mirror only to realize no one from the original convoy was around. What I did notice however, was a large police presence. They were heavily concentrated by the Ames Street off-ramp, where I'd just happened to get off.

Once I'd determined there were cops all over the place, while approaching the stoplight I decided I would just take my rump home instead of hitting that last bar. About a foot from the light, which was red at the time, I turned on my left turn signal. As soon as I did that and turned the corner a patrol car made a U-turn then proceeded to pull me over. As the officer approached my truck I noticed many other police vehicles pulling up around me. I was like, "What the fuck, I'm going to jail... Dammit man!" The officer walks up to the driver's side window and taps on it, all the while signaling me to roll down the window. I do so and the first thing he asks, "Do you know why I pulled you over?" I responded with, "No." He said, "You failed to signal 50 feet from the light. License and registration please." In my head I knew this was a bullshit reason and excuse to pull me over. For me, the real reason I was pulled over was for driving while black. Profiling at its best presented itself that night.

As the officer talked to me through the window he hesitated for a second while scanning the inside of my truck then, out of nowhere, he says,

"Where is it?"

I just stood there staring at him like he'd lost his mind then replied,

"Excuse me sir, what are you talking about? Where is what?"

"The weed, the weed! I smell it, where is it? Please step out of the vehicle and wait by the back of the truck while I take a look. Do you have any weapons or anything else I might find inside the vehicle? Where are the drugs located inside the truck because there is clearly an aroma of marijuana permeating your vehicle?"

At this point I was ignoring the officer. I knew I had weed in the truck, but I also had a few bags of cocaine. No way was I saying anything else or giving him permission to search my vehicle. So, instead I said, "I am not giving you permission to search my truck."

The officer replied, "We don't need your permission because we have probable cause due to the heavy stench of marijuana inside the vehicle. I knew that even a person with limited abilities would have no trouble smelling it and finding it."

By this time my heart is in my throat and I'm becoming more and more nervous. While I'm watching them search my truck I observe them pulling out the bag I kept the weed in. As the officer drops it on the hood of the patrol car he says, "You wanna guess what I just found? I hesitate in responding to his question and before I can say a word another officer yells out, "BINGO! Looky what we have here. It seems we have a bit of cocaine along with all that weed. What the hell were you gonna do, have a party?"

He continues with his sarcastic rhetoric for a few more minutes and says, "Turn around and place your hands on the car. I am going to search you. Are there any sharp objects in your pocket, anything I might cut myself on? I am placing you under arrest for Criminal Possession of Marijuana and Criminal Possession of a Controlled Substance."

Then, he places me in hand cuffs and puts me in the patrol car. There were so many cops around you would've thought they'd found Bin Laden or the catch of the century. My mind was racing, and I had no idea what to do at that point. My wife was in Jamaica and wouldn't be able to work on getting me out until she returned. Plus, it would be difficult to get in touch with her considering it would be an international call and I knew her phone would probably be off quite a bit to avoid the exorbitant phone charges.

After processing, I was given permission to make a phone call. I had no choice but to call my aunt whom I love dearly, though I seldom call her cause she never answers her damn phone. I always said I hope I'm never in an emergency or life and death situation because If I had to rely on her to pick up the phone or respond to a text message or voicemail I could be waiting for hours or days before she got back to me. By then, I could be dead!

Anyway, I shake my head and chuckle true to form, once I received my free call, I called her, and of course, there was no answer. I stood by the phone dialing her number over and over for at least 30 minutes until her daughter finally picked up.

By this time, I am a bit perturbed, which in retrospect I really had no right to be, since the reason I was calling was because I had gotten myself into trouble. At the time however, I didn't care, and my only thought was about getting out of jail. Thinking back, I realize this was all a part of the lessons I needed to learn. I had no patience and therefore, this was one attribute I desperately needed to work on. Anyhow, after speaking with my aunt, I felt that I had wasted my time calling because there was really nothing she could do at the time. She couldn't bail me out because she didn't have the money and all I could do was ask her to try and get in touch with my wife.

I had been in jail for two days before connecting with my wife and boy oh boy did she have an ear-full for me. As you can imagine the last thing I wanted to hear was that shit seeing I had enough on my mind with the pending charges. All I wanted her to do was find out what my bail was and hire me a lawyer. Finally, two long weeks and two court dates later I was finally released on bail.

The first court date was my arraignment for which they did not issue bail. I was sent back to my cell after court with a *No Bail, No Release* clause. The next court date, which was my bail application hearing, I was given bail in the amount of $10,000 bond or $5,000 cash. Finally, at least I had been given a sum to work with. It was time to find a bail bondsman and get the hell out of this hellhole.

Being out on bail was an extremely distressing time for me because of all the uncertainty surrounding my case. I had no idea how it was all going to play out. Meanwhile, the sentencing laws were changing constantly, and I knew that more and more people were receiving alternative to incarceration sentences. Programs were established and completing one could get a felony reduced to a misdemeanor.

My lawyer worked out a deal with the DA to have me participate in Drug Court called The Judicial Diversion Program. Participating in the program meant completing an intensive 18-month inpatient drug rehabilitation program. It meant I would be assigned someone from the court system who would be in touch with my program counselor. These two would communicate with regards to my progress and the notes would be relayed to the Judge. Therefore, if I became uncooperative, tried to leave the program before completion, was caught with contraband or did not obey the rules the judge in my case would be notified and I would have to go back before the judge.

Then the program would be stripped away from me and whatever my original sentence was would be enforced.

After weighing all my options, I decided to go with the rehab program. They would send me to a facility somewhere outside Rochester and I wouldn't know which one until I arrived there. Once the program was complete they would send me back to Rochester where I would go to a halfway house for three months, then transition home. Meanwhile I'd be going to drug court every so often until the day I graduated from the program. After mulling all this over it seemed like a no-brainer; I'd go to the program and the only jail time I'd see was the time I'd spend sitting in the county jail waiting to be transported to the Rehabilitation Facility. I immediately said, "DEAL!"

The day of sentencing, the judge gave me a lengthy speech about the program I was being sentenced to and how it was an opportunity to get myself together and how it was a great alternative to incarceration. He drove home the point of how grateful I should be and how I'd better take advantage of this time and be productive with my period of rehabilitation. The judge also made it clear that if I was to come back before him because I messed up this opportunity he was providing, he would resort back to my original prison sentence.

Once his lengthy speech was finally over, it was time for sentencing. The Judge said, "What is your name for the record?" I replied, "Terrell Brady." He then says, "Mr. Brady for the charges of Criminal Possession of a

Controlled Substance in the 3rd degree and Illegal Possession of Marijuana in the 2nd degree, I am sentencing you to a period of two to four years, a minimum of two years and a maximum not to exceed four years. This sentence would be imposed if unsuccessful or non-completion of The Judicial Diversion Program which I am allowing you to participate in. Upon completion of this program your felony will be reduced to a misdemeanor and you will not have to report to state parole. I wish you good luck Mr. Brady and remember I do not want to see you under any circumstance unless it's to hand you your certificate of completion."

His words resonated with me from that moment until the day I completed the program. I was sent to a facility in Liverpool, NY, a suburb of Syracuse. I was thankful I would be so close to home. All the other facilities were four or more hours away. I knew if I were sent any further I wouldn't receive any visitors. I knew I'd need a visit or two to get me through my time there. Just seeing a familiar face helps tremendously in getting you through that time away from home. I couldn't have imagined going the entire time without seeing anyone in my family. Talk about a strain on your psyche when you never see family or friends and it gets awfully lonely.

Once we arrived we were greeted by rehabilitation center counselors. They said, "Welcome to 820 River Street Rehab Center." I immediately wondered why they called it 820 River Street considering the address was something totally different. The evening staff seemed to be nice and approachable. They gave us our room assignments and the rules of the facility and allowed us to go to our rooms to wash up and go to bed.

As soon as I stepped foot inside the facility I felt I had made the right choice. There were no bars or fences, we could wear our own clothes, which meant no uniforms and we were free to walk around and could even go outside. So, as I gauged my surroundings I determined I would do exactly what the judge had suggested and make the best of my time there.

Wanting to avoid the same pitfalls as before, I prepared for my second release ahead of time. I decided there were several things I could do to ensure that when I arrived home, I wouldn't waste as much time trying to figure out my next steps. Therefore, while still inside, I began to heavily advocate for myself in getting things accomplished. With the assistance of my prison counselor I set goals to ensure I was being productive and learning new skills in the process.

During this process, it is important not to give up at the first sign of difficulty. Guards and counselors have seen it all and when you make your plans for advancement known to them, they take it with a grain of salt. They want to see a certain level of persistence and grit before they start investing time into your goals. Advocating for yourself is no small task while detained, and it took several meetings before my counselor realized how serious and sincere I was in trying to change my life for the better. She told me that as long as she saw me working towards my goals she would assist me. That was all the motivation I needed and when preparing for upcoming meetings with her, I did my part by researching opportunities. Instead of coming to my meetings empty handed, I came ready to present valuable information.

During one of our sessions my counselor asked me about my career interests. I told her I was interested in obtaining a bachelor's in Human Resource Management or Business Administration. Later, nearing the time of my release, I asked her if we could sit down and fill out my FASFA (financial aid) forms so I wouldn't have to delay my start date for college. I also made her aware that I was interested in doing an internship at a local company and asked if it was somehow possible the facility would allow me off the compound a few hours a week. After our many conversations, my counselor told me that she had never met anyone so driven and focused on filling every minute with productive work-related activities.

Several months had passed when my counselor approached me about a group of older gentlemen who were pursuing their General Education Diploma (GED) through the Board of Cooperative Educational Services (BOCES). She said the program instructor was seeking three tutors to assist the gentlemen with reading comprehension and math and would I be interested. I gave her a resounding YES and asked for more details.

Now, of course I wondered why, of all the guys in the facility, she had asked me to be one of the three tutors to fill this assignment. Then I snapped to and said to myself, "Who in the hell cares? It doesn't matter as long as I'm out of here a few times a week and can help my *Bros* in the process. Seemed like a win-win to me and oh yeah, it would be a resume builder too."

So, off I went to help the guys who were also hoping to accomplish something better for themselves and improve their situation upon release. This would give them a greater chance at obtaining employment and or in pursuing higher education. Doing this also gave me a sense of pride in saying, "Hey I helped that brother get his GED and now the sky is the limit for him." Knowing that I assisted someone else in accomplishing their goals is the best feeling in the world. I believe we are all here to help one another achieve success in some form or another. It's only right that we push each other to greatness and in becoming the best we can possibly be.

Following each tutoring session, the guys would continue their work upon their return to the housing unit and oftentimes they would come to me with questions. They needed help getting through some of the math problems and I would work through it with them. Another reason this helped me was because it taught me patience. Patience is something I had always lacked.

Once I realized that God was working with me and through me I shouted, "Thank you Father God for

111

continuing to work on me in making me a better man, servant, and brother to those around me." Just having the know how to work through those word problems and actually teach someone the steps in solving math equations was very rewarding. Teaching others requires patience and God knows I needed to develop more of it. Everyone isn't in the same place academically, though with persistence and hard work, can eventually get there, but working through the problems with others allowed me to see the growth within myself.

During this time, I started noticing changes taking place within me. There was a point where I had gotten burned so many times that I couldn't care less about helping others. It didn't matter how badly they needed the help, how important it was to them, or whether I was the only one able to help them. Either way I just didn't care. I felt so used and taken advantage of that I didn't want to extend my hand in service ever again. In essence, I was done with people.

But tutoring these older men just did something to improve my spirit. To see them come alive as they were doing homework, or to witness that light bulb come on once I had explained a math concept to them, was very rewarding and made me happy. I didn't know I could feel this way while doing a service for someone else. I began to ask God what was going on with me. How could I possibly feel good about doing something for which I wasn't receiving any material benefits?

Then God placed a couple of scriptures on my heart pertaining to the service of others; Matthew 5:16 , "In the same way, let your light shine before **others**, that they may see your good deeds and glorify your Father in heaven." And Mark 10:44-45, "And whoever wants to be first must be slave of all. For even the Son of Man did not come to be served, but to serve, and to give his life as a ransom for many." 1 Peter 4:10, "Each one should use whatever gift he has received to serve others, faithfully administering God's grace in its various forms." Then it all began to make sense. It was because of the service I was providing the guys and not looking for anything in return that I felt good in my spirit. It was me giving of myself purely from my heart.

Not only did I enjoy helping the guys with their class work I realized I had a talent and skill I could use for good. It hadn't dawned on me until some months into the tutoring sessions that I was in possession of a skill that could benefit others. Never would I have even considered anything I knew as a potential tool to assist others in their mission to better themselves. My lack of self-esteem had never allowed me to recognize my potential until that moment.

I finally felt some sense of growth and awareness going on within me and was happy that my outlook was beginning to change. Others recognized a drastic change in me as well. I can honestly say that this marked an official period of transformation and an awakening I couldn't quite explain.

I used to sit and try to analyze what was going on, even though I knew deep down, that I was simply tired of the life I had been living. If I wanted different results I needed to do things differently. And that's exactly what I began to do.

In addition to working with the guys in the GED program through BOCES, I began to intern in the HR department at the People's Equal Action and Community Effort or P.E.A.C.E. Inc. Which is a Children's Head Start Program. I had envisioned doing something like this once I arrived home but was presented with the opportunity to do so while still in the program. I had been working on it with my counselor and thankfully it worked out.

My counselor was required to advocate for me and therefore I had to prove my value. So, to be accepted as one of their interns I had to interview with the program director just as if I was going for a real job interview. I needed to explain to the interviewer what skills I possessed and what skills I was trying to obtain or what I was trying to get out of my internship. I presented my resume and simply made it clear that I wanted to learn all aspects and functions of the Human Resources Department from recruiting and interviewing to benefits and training.

The director looked over my resume and asked a few questions about my previous employment and my time as a business owner. That conversation sparked other discussions. After our *chat* so to speak, and I call it a *chat* because where interviews are concerned, it started out as a formal interview, but ended on an informal note. We began joking and laughing and talking about family and leisure activities etc. I know employers sometimes use that tactic to see if a perspective employee or intern will fit into a workplace culture, but for me this was very different, and I had never been in that style of interview before.

Before I left, the director decided to show me around the building and fill me in on some of the duties that would be required of me. I was told that I was not officially hired until my counselor informed me as such. A recommendation would be presented in front of the team, but the director didn't see why, out of all the candidates interviewed, I wouldn't be the one chosen for the position.

The next Wednesday I received a call that I would begin starting on the following Monday at 8 a.m. I was extremely pleased because that meant things were beginning to turn around for me. I would be doing something I wanted to and finally getting a chance to be productive and learn a new craft. I breathed a sigh of relief as I could see my future beginning to take shape. This opportunity lifted a mountain of weight off my shoulders. I started seeing my life in a much different light than when I first began the program. The best part was that the uncertainty about my future started to go away.

Chapter Twenty-One

RELATIONSHIPS

As the date for my second release drew closer, I was really looking forward to getting home to my wife. I wanted to show her the new and improved me. I was ready to get back and try to make things work between the two of us. I had not been a great husband though my wife was a sweetheart. In my damaged state I had damaged her. But now, I was going to do my best to repair some of the damage and try to rebuild a life with her.

After years spent running the streets, arguing, fighting, and infidelity, I was finally ready to try and make it work. I felt it was time to build a family the way I should've in the first place. I finally envisioned us whole and complete, a wife and kids as one unit, not separate parts of a whole as it had been before.

Looking back, I now know that I jumped into my first marriage at the wrong time in life and was clearly ill-prepared. Marriage was extremely difficult for me and I was too immature to take such solemn vows, let alone live up to them. I should have waited. I am sad nonetheless that I was unable to live up to the challenges of marriage, and that I couldn't find a way to keep my ex-wife happy. My inability to make our marriage work is one of my biggest regrets.

If I could do it all over again I would do things much differently. I now know that being open and honest is key to a good relationship and I finally understand the importance of effective communication. People need to really get to know each other and get a clear understanding of each other's wants and needs. I also now understand the value of being faithful to the person you've committed to.

I used to try to buy my ex-wife's happiness which was a huge mistake. I would cheat, get caught, and then try to buy my way back into her good graces by giving her gifts. This never solved any of our issues and instead it just delayed the inevitable for years. We were so different from one another and neither of us was happy. In the end, though we lived in the same house, we were living separate lives.

Though I understand it now, it still enrages me whenever I think back to what pushed us over the edge. I've accepted where I went wrong in the marriage, but the most infuriating part of this equation is that I had reached a point where I wanted to make it work. Unfortunately, it was too late.

I had been locked up for about a year following my second arrest. During that entire time my wife had been strategizing on divorcing me as quickly as possible upon my release. She never once informed me of her plan, though I had asked her for months about her intentions. She reassured me we would work through our issues and try to make the marriage work. She had been lying to me the entire time and instead had contacted a lawyer to start divorce proceedings. Had she told me, at least I could've better prepared myself for my homecoming, but she chose not to.

Instead, she announced on my second day home that she had filed for divorce. I was furious because of the lies, but also because she kept asking me for money. For some reason she thought I had all this money stashed away whereas any money I did have saved I had sent her in the hopes that we were going to work out our marriage.

Later, I found out that while I was locked up someone whom I'd considered a good friend was making moves on my wife. I was furious! I was not only met with divorce papers but with information that there was some type of inappropriate relationship going on between the two of them.

I instantly thought that my wife did this with my friend as a way of getting back at me for all the infidelity throughout our marriage. But for it to be with someone I considered a friend and had asked to look out while I would be gone was like a slap in the face. If it was a stranger, I'd accept it without question but to be sleeping with someone I considered a friend wasn't something I was willing to let go of immediately.

I found out secretly he wanted my life, why I'll never be able to figure out. My house, my wife, my cars simply everything. His kids would come over and they'd steal my sneakers and anything of mine that wasn't nailed down. He made it a point to tell my wife bad things about me in an effort to get with her, and at the end of the day it worked.

I felt compelled to address this news with my friend once I found out the truth. Deek and I went over there with the intention of confronting him and putting the beats to him. But as I talked to him and asked questions all he did was back pedal and make excuses and apologize. The real reason I wanted to go over there wasn't to talk or ask questions but to fight. I began to ask myself what the fuck for? He is a non-factor in my life and a fucking bum that she chose to have an affair with. He will always be a bum and if I fought him over this yes, I would've felt better, but it would've also said I wanted to fight for our marriage, but I had reached a point where I absolutely did not. I came to realize it was a lose-lose situation for me. On the one hand here was someone I had trusted and called friend and on the other there was my wife. Both were complicit and knew I would never be able to look at either of them in the same way ever again.

For years I held a lot of resentment towards her because she had kicked me while I was down and at my lowest point and was having some type of relationship with my friend while I was locked up. I literally had nothing; no money, no place to live, and no prospects. I had to hurry up and find a place to live because she

120

wanted me to leave. Yes, she wanted me out of the very house I had put all my blood sweat and tears into. I had invested a lot of money and physical labor into that house only to be put out like some homeless guy going door to door asking for handouts.

I felt completely defeated. Why was she being so mean and vindictive? I know I had put her through a lot of hurt and pain over the years, and though I had strong feelings for her, I hadn't done a very good job expressing them. This latest development however eliminated any thoughts I had left of fighting to get her back. In addition, once I moved, I found out the real reason she wanted me out of the house so quickly was because she was dating another guy as well. So, she had essentially moved on with her life long before I was completely out the picture.

Rage consumed me but because I was in no position to do anything to fight back it just crushed me. Normally I would lash out or retaliate in some way to hurt her as much if not more than she had hurt me. Though I gave it some thought, I concluded that getting worked up would solve nothing. I did not want to give her any leverage to use against me while I was still going through drug court. After all, she had called the police on me before and probably wouldn't hesitate to do it again.

Besides, I did not want my son to watch us go through a messy ordeal. At the end of the day, the new me wanted to show him that a man can act like a gentleman no matter what the situation. So, I decided I wasn't gonna fight for the house or any of its contents, because in the end, I wanted to make sure my son didn't have to go through an even larger transition by being uprooted from the only home he knew. Though I also had a daughter, she was no longer living at home and wouldn't be affected by the divorce in the same way that he would.

In the long run I learned much from this failed marriage. After all, I did not have good examples growing up and had no idea what real love looked like. My marriage, though painful, taught me a lot about the right and wrong way to treat and love on a woman.

Chapter Twenty-Two

MY DARKEST HOUR

I became extremely bitter while going through our divorce which manifested itself into an eventual bout of depression. At one point the depression got so bad that I didn't even want to leave my apartment. Days upon days went by where I just sat there in the dark. There were many days when I could barely eat. I felt hopeless and was in such a funk that my friends literally had to come by and drag me out of the house, just so I could get some fresh air. Nothing was fun anymore.

As I think back I can say I am happy I had friends that cared enough about me to constantly check on me. I had no desire to do anything or be around people. Heck I didn't even want to be bothered by my best friend. I remember not answering the phone a few days and my friend Deek just showed up and dragged me out the house. Boy how I fussed and cussed and called him annoying, but this did not stop him from being a friend. At the end of the day it was just what the doctor ordered and I'm grateful to all my friends for checking on me.

I had no idea that depression could hold such a grip on you. It got to a point where I completely lost sight of who I was and what I wanted. It took me a while to dissect the time my ex-wife and I had spent together, and to reflect on what led to the failed relationship. I had to recognize the part I had played in all of it. No more finger pointing without looking at myself first! The more I reflected on our failed marriage, the more I realized how much of it had been my fault.

Eventually admitting to my part in the demise of our relationship was the beginning of my spiritual growth and healing. In the long run, the painful divorce became one of the best lessons learned along my journey towards emotional maturity and in finding true love.

Chapter Twenty-Three

THE COURAGE TO SEEK HELP

In time I recognized that the first step in rebuilding my life was in learning how to love and most importantly, how to properly love a new mate. Because of the pain I had just endured during the inevitable divorce and because of the poor examples I had growing up, I knew I needed to talk this thing through.

I didn't feel I could talk to any of my friends about all this and felt I may need professional guidance. I desperately wanted someone to help me get back on track and to help shed light on the continuous string of problems I'd been having. After wrestling with myself for some time, I finally made the decision to go to counseling.

This was one of the hardest decisions I'd made to date because I had always shied away from speaking to strangers about *ME* let alone any problems I was having. Not to mention that in the black community, counseling is not something promoted, nor encouraged, and is often referred to as something only the weak, the rich, or the mentally ill do.

Furthermore, I remember my mother telling me "Terrell don't you go outside this house talking about what's going on in here." Which is partly why it took me years to build up the courage to talk to someone I didn't know. I had to overcome all these stereotypes before I could take the steps to talk to someone about my desire to be a better man.

I finally took the plunge and made an appointment to see a counselor. First, I jumped online and began to research counselors, then I proceeded to call and see who was taking new clients with my insurance. I must say, it was one of the most nerve-wracking things I have ever done. Here I was about to go into a room and spill my guts. I was secretly hoping against all odds that I would have the courage to open up and that I wouldn't withhold my feelings.

My first session was all about getting familiar with one another and her attempts at making me feel comfortable. She asked me if there was any one thing I felt I wanted to focus on. I didn't know how to answer the question because I felt I needed help in many areas, but because of what I had recently been through, I told her relationships. For some reason that popped into my head immediately. That area of my life was a real struggle and it took my divorce to recognize this.

I told her I felt I was *damaged* goods and we shared a laugh. Little did she know I was being serious. I had no idea what a healthy relationship looked like. No way did I want to emulate the relationships I'd seen growing up. My family was nothing like the Cosby's, or any other T.V. family for that matter!

After just a few sessions, things started to make sense to me. I now know why I handled situations the way I did in relationships. Seems cliché but it all stems from my childhood and the things I witnessed. Without realizing it I was basically mimicking the tattered relationships I'd seen growing up. In addition to that I guess I took on the role of caretaker. So, if I saw someone in need of help I would go out of my way to help them even at the expense of my own feelings, happiness, financial well-being, and my emotional stability. My counselor told me the reason I did this was because of all the abuse I'd seen at home between my mother and father. Instinctively, I always wanted to intervene in the beatings my mom had endured at the hand of my father.

Examining and reflecting on these behaviors made the counseling sessions all worthwhile. I recommend it to anyone who is trying to discover what makes them tick. Speaking from experience it really improved my mental health. Though counseling is typically frowned upon in the African-American community, I for one will not continue to promote this line of thinking and instead, I strongly recommend finding a counselor you can trust. In fact, many African-Americans have suffered so much trauma and abuse over the years, that learning to deal with our emotions is extremely valuable in moving towards building strong, healthy relationships.

Lastly, we discussed emotions and how to deal with them especially in terms of dealing with death.

Throughout my life I have always found it difficult to show emotion and shedding a tear even more difficult. I believe I have been through so much in my life that I have become numb to tragedy, death, and traumatic things in general. I didn't even cry when my father passed away, when my favorite uncle passed away, nor when my own son died.

Honestly, I have yet to really grieved the death of my father, uncle, grandparents, and son. At times I sit back and think about it but can't seem to come up with a valid reason. I am saddened by their untimely departure from this earth so that can't be the reason. I know it doesn't make me less of a man to cry while grieving, but I just can't bring myself to shed tears as a means of letting those emotions out. Sometimes I think about it and say to myself that I need a good cry, just one good tear flowing session to cleanse my soul from all the hurt and pain I have bottled up over the last 40 some years. Maybe one day...

One of the biggest challenges I still face, is that of grieving the death of my son. Many days I sit back and think about him. I swear I miss him and my heart truly aches because I often blame myself for his death. I tell myself that if it wasn't for my lifestyle and the things he'd seen growing up maybe he would be alive today.

He was a good kid, extremely smart, and athletic. I made sure he did not have to face any of the challenges I endured growing up. He went to well-reputed suburban schools and wasn't exposed to many of the challenges a lot of urban youth face and he had many more

128

opportunities to excel. At school he was exposed to a different lifestyle, so I didn't have to concern myself with him getting into too much trouble. Every child gets into some trouble, but my concerns for him were minimal.

So, while I'm talking to the counselor, telling her about my son she asks why I feel so much guilt. I began to explain, "One day I'm in the basement weighing some weed for a customer and my son comes downstairs to wash a load of clothes. He had no idea I was down there until he heard me rustling around in the utility room. We had a room I would normally lock in the basement where I kept all my tools, paint, paint thinner or chemicals for the most part and things of that nature, and sometimes I would stash my weed in this room temporarily until I could move it to the cool out." My son yelled, "Dad is that you, do you need help?" I respond, "Yeah Squirt it's me, no I'm fine I'll be out in a minute." Now as I'm doing this I'm saying to myself the entire time don't forget to lock the door. I leave out the house rushing, forgetting to lock the door. Later I found out that my son went back into the basement after I had left and found my weed stash.

I was so upset with myself for not locking the door. Kids are inquisitive, so I couldn't fault him for that. I blamed myself for having the weed in the house and for having to hustle as a means of financial support. I never wanted to expose him to that. It was bad enough that I was running the streets but now he had confirmation of what I had been doing.

129

All these years my son had been in a protected environment. I hustled so that he didn't have to, and up until this point, he'd lived the exact life I had laid out for him. If it weren't for me being sloppy he would never have seen the weed in the house. He looked up to me and so naturally him seeing me hustle gave validation to that behavior.

Although he had seen first-hand what I had been involved in, he had decided he wanted to go into law enforcement. In college, he majored in criminal justice and it did my heart proud. While enrolled, he started working at a juvenile detention center. The boys loved him and all that he did for them. During that time, he also had obtained his security license and had a few gigs as a bouncer. Since my son was working security, he worked out almost daily. He had gotten huge and really strong. One day, simply because of his size and strength, someone he knew asked him to come along with him to offer him protection while he robbed a drug dealer. The guy thought that because of my son's size, it would be intimidating to the drug dealer and that he'd be more apt to give up the marijuana without a fight. Against his better judgment, my son went. When they arrived, the dealer was unexpectedly armed and fired shots at them.

When I got the news of my son's murder, I was devastated and completely shocked as all he'd ever talked about was going into law enforcement. He had made a stupid mistake in hopes of making a quick buck and it had gotten him killed. I couldn't help but think I had opened the door for his behavior to seem acceptable. The adage of, *do as I say and not as I do* is a lie. Children emulate what they see and mimic those they look up to.

I suppose because my son was the *one black* male I felt I could directly mold and influence, I was determined that he not become a statistic. But if I'm honest with myself he did, which is why he was shot and killed before the age of 25. That makes his death so much harder to deal with. No father wants their child to die before them. It's not the natural course of life and It hurts!

Knowing oneself is empowering and it is something I would love to master. I must say I have grown by leaps and bounds and a step forward is better than no steps, but I know I still have quite a way to go.

Chapter Twenty-Four

SOCIAL ENTREPRENEURSHIP

Determined to not become anything like my father, I vowed not to repeat history. Instead, I looked at every fucked-up thing he ever did and decided to do just the opposite. Terrible experiences growing up can produce a new crop of bad experiences for generations to come. Unhealthy habits left uncorrected are the premise for generational curses. Determined to break this cycle, I decided to make it my business to teach and enlighten the younger men in my family, so I might help them avoid the same mistakes I had made. I learned that this is essential to their growth and development. If we ever wanted to become productive leaders, I needed to learn important life lessons that would contribute to the growth and development of our young men.

I knew I had to start in my home first; with my own kids, my nephew and my niece. I made it a point to talk to them during our outings. We talked about whatever they had going on in their lives and discussed any relationship stuff, any teenage anxiety they may be experiencing or had questions about.

Another topic we discussed relatively often was that of finances. I hadn't learned anything of value about money when I was growing up and knew I did not want to pass that generational curse on. I vowed that my kids would know about money, how to save and build a

132

relationship with a bank or credit union, whichever they chose that best fit their needs. I couldn't see not showing them a better way even if at times, they didn't really want to pay attention. I continued to pass on information I had learned on my own or taught to me, seeing it had not been taught in my parent's home.

I eventually became part owner of a restaurant and one of our goals was to hire local youth to work there. We hoped to provide them mentorship and teach them transferable skills. Our plan was to provide them with some life experience and train them to earn a living wage. Many times, I had one on one conversations with the students pertaining to their lives and what they were going through as well as what they wanted to do with the rest of their lives.

Because I hadn't received much guidance growing up, having the chance to discuss life and give helpful information to these young people did my heart proud. Just to have someone you can trust to bounce ideas off or listen to in helping one to avoid the pitfalls of life. I would have welcomed that growing up and it probably would have meant the difference in being successful a lot sooner. Instead I had to struggle through unnecessary trials.

Providing young people with the tools they need to avoid major mistakes and bad decisions brings me immense joy. After many lessons and a lot of trial and error, I believe it is now my obligation to impact those generations after me.

Chapter Twenty-Five

ADDRESSING CYNICS

I'd been home for about month or so the second time around when I started running into more and more family members. On more than one occasion I overheard whispers, "Rell home but let's see how long his ass stay out this time." And, "I don't know why he can't seem to get his shit together." One of my cousins told me that when my grandparents found out I was home from prison, they were heard saying, "I wonder if he gonna get it right this time and how long do we have him back for?"

All this chatter and commentary saddened me, but it also lit a spark under my ass to get it together and prove everybody wrong. Not just to show them but to prove to myself that I had the ability to get it right. The whispering, the lack of support, and their belief in my downfall provided me with the fuel to make a successful run at this *changing my life* thing.

Their skepticism is the very reason I decided to get involved in so many things. I felt I had no choice but to do well and be recognized for it. I completed my degree, worked in my field of study for a year, then opened my own restaurant. Upon reaching each milestone people slowly began to acknowledge how well I was doing. Some even cheered me on and told me to keep up the good work. At times I thought they were being insincere and just blowing smoke up my ass, so I wouldn't pay them any attention. Especially because the same unsupportive people were the ones whispering and saying negative things behind my back. Either way, I simply continued with the road map I had laid out for myself.

While working in my field of study, I found myself in a position I truly enjoyed. However, within the year a good friend of mine called me proposing a potential business opportunity. He suggested we take over the lease on an existing restaurant. He and I had often discussed wanting to open a bar but never a restaurant. I must admit, I was intrigued and felt this was along the lines of something I'd always wanted to do. The prospect had essentially fallen into our laps and he believed we should take advantage of it. Though the place needed a major facelift, we decided to go for it. After all, it already had a full bar and kitchen and lots of available parking.

I knew going in we would need to sink a bit of money into the place to get it up and running and presentable to the public. Nonetheless, a year later we were open and ready to receive customers. A lot of time and work went into getting that place up and running and doing so was a major accomplishment. I remember working my eight-hour shift then going over to the restaurant to help with the renovations.

We had been open for some time before some members of my family visited the restaurant for dinner and cocktails. I guess it took them a while to come around because maybe they couldn't believe I had what it takes to be part owner of a restaurant. I don't know but to see the amazement on their faces as they walked in spoke volumes. While talking with them, I couldn't help thinking to myself, "Yep I did this with no help or support from any of you. Some of my family members, who should've been supportive and encouraging, were instead waiting for me to fail. It was as if they were hoping to be able to say, "I told you so."

Nevertheless, I took a chance on the business. It took some time to build up a clientele but once we did we gained a good reputation in the community. As people came in to dine we also began to develop relationships with our patrons many of whom became regulars. We developed a stellar reputation for amazing food especially our wings, Cajun fish fries, steaks, and our delicious jambalaya.

Our first year open we put on a Thanksgiving meal and a Christmas spread for the homeless. We gathered donations to fund the dinners and we enlisted many volunteers to help us with preparations and the serving. We did this every year thereafter. We also offered up our space for funeral repass services and fund-raising events.

The relationships we built at the restaurant will last us a lifetime. During our time open we practically built another family. I call them my *Charleston House* family. I love them all dearly and they looked after me as if we had the same blood running through our veins. They were no more or less my relatives than my real blood relatives except I could count on my *Charleston House* family more and I saw them more. We built relationships with dignitaries and the mayor who was a regular customer of ours. We often hosted Senators, County Legislators, City Councilmen and others. Our customer base consisted of a wide variety of people in various positions. Some affluent people, some white collar, and some blue collar. If you came into the restaurant we tried our best to make everyone feel welcome and as if they were at home with family.

Recognizing how important these relationships were, was a critical moment for me because there was once a point in my life where I saw myself as a loner who needed no one. How wrong I was. Believing this for as long as I had only crippled me. Thinking this way was nothing but a fallacy taught and handed down throughout my years growing up.

Each of us has a network of people. Building relationships allows us to expand that network. If I know someone who can help you accomplish a task or goal, then my relationship with this person becomes a benefit to you. Now you have just tapped into my network which in turn extends yours and vice-versa. The next time I need something done, someone in your network may be able to assist. This is how we mutually expand our networks.

Some call this paying it forward. I help you accomplish something and then somewhere down the line you'll recommend me to someone else. Or I'll help you with your car and you'll help me with my roof, for example. It is so important to build up a network of people we enjoy being around and working with. For a returning citizen, you may need to build a new network or at the very least, eliminate people from your previous one. The goal is to surround yourself with positive influences, while also becoming a positive role model yourself.

Chapter Twenty-Six

LOOKING FOR LOVE

I eventually met a young woman with whom I thought I had a lot in common. To my dismay, over time it became clear that we just could not get along. This caused me to further question what I might be doing that prevented us from getting to a place where we could see eye to eye. What part did I play in our many arguments and what part did she play? Why did I dislike speaking to her? I felt it became impossible to have conversations because they always ended with me feeling like I had said something wrong. One wrong word and the arguing commenced. I called it an argument while she called it a conversation. This left me wondering how yelling, raised voices, and tense responses could ever be considered conversations. But hey what do I know? I was never one to engage in heated discussions because in my experience they always ended badly. Someone always said something they later regretted, and the discussion ended up going in an unintended direction.

This relationship, though destined to fail, also taught me a lot about inter-personal communication skills, once again, one of which is patience. I learned to listen more and speak less. If I simply paused and listened to what was being said I was better off. Whether the conversation was about an issue that needed fixing or about her wants and needs, paying close attention helped close the communication gap and allowed me to respond appropriately.

Unfortunately, the relationship didn't last but what I gained from it was invaluable. I had taken a step in the right direction though I couldn't help but wonder what the heck I might be doing to constantly attract the same type of woman. It appeared I always got involved with women who were just as damaged as I was; those that were needy and wanted someone to take care of them emotionally and financially.

My relationships were never built on equal footing. There was no, give and take, in any sense of the word. Maybe this is the reason I sought outside companionship while married. Something I never should've done yet in retrospect, now realize that failing to communicate my wants and needs to my partner undoubtedly contributed to my promiscuity.

I realized I still needed time to figure myself out before I could find someone I truly enjoyed being with. I wanted to find someone without all the extra drama and someone who didn't need me to take care of them. I just couldn't go through another relationship like that and instead, wanted someone who had my back just as much as I had theirs. I wanted to develop a relationship with someone who meets most of my wants and needs and who cares about my wellbeing.

Meanwhile, in the back of my mind I feared I might not find that person anytime soon. Did this person even exist and was she out there as a perfect match for me? I just knew there had to be someone because I believe God places at least one true match for every human on planet earth. So, with that in mind it would soon be time for me to try to find out who that might be.

Chapter Twenty-Seven

LOVE AT LAST

One November, a young lady I'd dated 20 years before reentered my life. Throughout the years we seemed to run into each other quite often and as time progressed I began to think it was a sign. She and I had never completely lost touch but to be quite honest some time had passed since the last run in. But perhaps there was a reason we kept running into each other. Was this a divine occurrence? Funny thing is I had been crushing on her all these years though I don't believe she ever knew it. From the very beginning I felt she was the one I was meant to be with, to grow old with, and with whom I could share special memories.

Throughout the years life happened and we both went through some things, though I did find myself calling or texting her periodically to see how she was doing. I would send her a random message just to say Hi and see how her week or day had gone. It would be so random that I knew she wouldn't be expecting it, but it was my way of letting her know she was on my mind.

During my divorce we talked quite often because that was a tough time in my life and she offered support and words of encouragement. I had no idea that she was also going through her own relational issues at that time because she kept the focus on me and never once tried to divert the focus on herself. She was truly a friend in every sense of the word. Who would've thought a few years would go by before we would reconnect on a different level.

Throughout our many conversations I made her aware of my criminal history, the time I had spent in prison and my many indiscretions while married, which was the main reason for my divorce. She never once judged or scolded me for it. She always listened and left me with some encouraging words. I started to see another side of her that I had not seen before. I was getting to know her heart.

As I look back on that time, I believe it was a needed period of growth and learning for each of us, so we could develop into our best selves. This was our moment and we had made our way back to each other at the perfect time in our lives.

As I continue to reflect I know that God had his hand on us the whole time. Who else would know what we needed to learn, experience, and change to make us better people. Who else but God would know my inner most heart's desire and would hear my prayers for the perfect mate. A mate that would start out as my friend first and someone whom I could talk to and relate with. Someone who'd seen me at my worst and still could accept me and believed that there was a better version of me.

As the days progressed and I spent more and more time with her, I began to see her inner beauty. Her spirit radiates kindness and service. Her willingness to help others and her passion for working with youth is what makes her so special to those around her. Seeing her smile puts a smile on my heart, which is something I've never felt before. In fact, I am experiencing many feelings for this woman that I have not experienced for any other. I want the world to know how my heart smiles now because of her. I no longer feel as though I am floating aimlessly through life. I am finally feeling alive. Daily I ask myself how it is possible to fall more and more in love with someone as the days progress. I feel myself wanting to spend more time with her and not wanting her to leave my side.

Just to sit and talk, pray, read the word and discuss it, laugh, and even be in each other's presence without getting on one another's nerves...means the world to me. To hold her and steal kisses, rub her back, hold her hand, kiss her forehead and her hands, to be able to bump into her while we are walking just to get close to her and touch her. These simple rituals are what draw me closer and closer to her.

After all I'd been through I never dreamt I'd be in a relationship where we both have many of the same thoughts, ambitions, and drive. We have a love for life, we're interested in traveling, and I've finally found someone who enjoys fishing as much as I do! We like jazz and are interested in trying new things... or at least not opposed to it, which I really appreciate. Most of all, having someone in my life who offers to help and who doesn't expect me to take care of everything, is a breath of fresh air. I don't mind putting in work, but it's nice to have someone who has your back.

Chapter Twenty-Eight

WEDDING BELLS

I suppose you're wondering what happened with that lovely lady I'd reunited with following a 20-year hiatus. As our relationship continued to blossom I eventually met her three daughters who range in ages from 20 to 25. At first, they had strong reservations about me. They were not used to seeing their mother dating or bringing any men friends around, so it was hard to fathom their mother seeing someone. I hear this is typical of situations involving children, particularly in cases where the main guardian has been single. Her oldest and youngest daughters accepted me a bit faster than her middle daughter did. The middle child made it clear that she wasn't trying to hear that her mother had a boyfriend period. No matter what was said or done she did not want to accept it.

One day we went on a little road trip to the casino to celebrate her youngest daughter's birthday and during the ride, there were many conversations and hints thrown up into the air. After some time listening to the girls' chattering on about their mother not needing to date anyone, I spoke up and asked them why they didn't think their mother deserved to be happy. I told them they were adults and it was time for their mother to have someone in her life to spoil her because she deserved to be spoiled. They told me that she is already spoiled because they spoil her. I explained that being spoiled by someone she calls her companion or mate is much different. It took some time to convince the girls that I had their mother's best interests at heart, and they eventually accepted me as part of their lives.

A few months later, I decided I would ask this wonderful new love to marry me. I believed it was time to take the next step in solidifying our relationship and in keeping things moving in the right direction. Before doing so however, I had to pull her most reluctant daughter aside to see how she felt about me asking her mother to marry me. She of course took the opportunity to grill me and presented me with a flurry of questions before giving me her answer. She finally said she wouldn't stand in our way. I asked her if she'd be attending the surprise engagement party we were planning. Her original response was, "You don't need me there." I told her that her mother wouldn't want to go through with this if all her children weren't in attendance. Then she said, "Ok I'll be there." I didn't fully believe her because she seemed so against it in the beginning and I still felt as though she didn't like me at all. But I didn't want to go through with everything without her children's blessing and without them being in attendance.

After speaking with her daughters, I decided that I would talk to the men in her family. In this relationship I wanted to do things differently from beginning to end. So, I decided I would take the old-fashioned approach to asking for a woman's hand in marriage. She had been wishing and hoping to have her family's blessing before I popped the big question.

With that in mind, and assistance from her oldest daughter, on Sunday January 22, 2017, I met with the men in her family to ask their permission for her hand in marriage. This experience was enlightening and one I will never forget. I was unaware as to what to expect once they arrived and we began talking. While setting up this meeting, I didn't have any unrealistic expectations. I told myself that if they showed up that would be great and if they welcomed me into the family that would be even better, but I had no clue what might happen.

After the guys interrogated me for a while, they unanimously gave me their seal of approval. I couldn't wait to tell her, so I pretended I needed a ride home because I'd had too much to drink. When she arrived, she was surprised and a little confused to see all the guys there with me. Everyone enthusiastically gave her their blessing. I never seen such a huge smile of her face until that moment.

On January 28, 2017, we had our first combined family gathering. There, I met more of her family and friends and my daughter also attended. Things went well, and I must say that I am happy to have been embraced and welcomed into the family. It is really comforting to feel so accepted by them.

On February 17, 2017 I asked the love of my life to marry me and she promptly accepted. This made me the happiest man on planet earth. On this day my fiancé's family, her oldest daughter, and her best friend helped me surprise her with an amazingly well-planned proposal! The day was made even more special because it was her oldest daughter's birthday and she allowed me to share the engagement celebration with her birthday celebration.

The day started out like any other, but as it progressed, several curve balls heightened my nervousness. For starters, my fiancé called to say she had been in a minor car accident, which meant someone else had to pick up the *birthday* cake for her daughter which was on the opposite side of town. I couldn't help but wonder if this was a sign of things to come.

The whole event had been planned under the guise of a birthday party for her oldest daughter. Amidst all the drama I was trying not to give her any indication of the surprise engagement we'd planned, which made me even more nervous. Her best friend helped me set up the room with candles in anticipation of the proposal. We decided to arrange them into a heart shape on the floor, so I could propose inside the formation. The tables were also covered with candles strategically placed to form hearts.

By now, all her friends and family were gathered in the room in anticipation of her arrival. It was taking her longer to arrive than expected, so I began to worry. While waiting, I took a walk to see if I could recruit some patrons to hand roses to her as she entered the venue. Thankfully, I ran into my godbrother, who helped me manage the situation, which relieved some of my stress.

Once she arrived, she was handed a dozen roses, one by one along her way to the party room. She didn't believe the roses were for her because the event was actually supposed to be in honor of her oldest daughter's birthday, who had secretly helped me plan the engagement.

When she entered the room, I was standing there within the heart-shaped candle formation holding two roses in my hand. When she opened the door, she was so taken off guard that she immediately turned around and walked back out into the hallway. Several people ran out to check on her and she eventually reentered the room.

I took her by the hand while she kept repeating, "Terrell what are you doing?" And lead her inside the candle formation. Once in place, she just kept looking down at the floor, refusing to make eye contact. I touched her chin and asked her to look at me. She didn't right away, but once she did, I asked her if she was ok then proceeded to tell her how I felt about her. John Legend's *So High*, played in the background, and once she became aware of it, she immediately recognized it, smiled, and said, "Oh wow that's our song!"

After I had finished speaking I bent down on one knee and was about to ask her to marry me when I realized my leg was straddling the lit candles. I quickly got up to adjust my position just in time to avoid catching fire. I grinned and thought to myself that the last thing I wanted was for everyone to remember how I'd caught on fire while trying to propose! I knew I'd never hear the end of it. So Finally, I asked her if she would do me the honor of being my wife and she said, "Yes!" I then placed the ring on her finger and gave her the biggest hug and kiss I could muster up.

This made me the happiest man alive. I thanked God for allowing my dream to come true. In my heart, I always knew we would be together one day, but didn't know when it would happen. I've heard it said often that everything happens in God's timing and only He knows when you are truly ready to receive your blessing.

So, begins a new chapter in our lives together. I have never been happier with any other woman. I tell everyone how my love for her has eliminated my desire for other women and I don't believe I have ever been able to say that with certainty until now. I am looking forward to our future together.

Chapter Twenty-Nine

STEPS TO TAKE PRIOR TO RELEASE

What I did leading up to my second release was make sure I had a viable plan in place. Where we fall short is in not making realistic plans. We end up getting caught up in the excitement of being out of confinement and forget that it's just the beginning. It's easy for everything you thought about and all your good intentions to go right out the window once life starts happening in real time. Writing out my plan and putting it to work allowed no room for getting back into the swing of old habits or hanging out with old friends who were still engaged in the same activities I had been prior to going on that long, unplanned *vacation*, so to speak.

Signing up for school was at the top of my list of things to accomplish. Because I didn't want to miss out on the upcoming semester I approached a couple of different colleges to see what they offered in terms of curriculum. I also wanted to know which college would accept me regardless of my past and thankfully I found one.

The next thing on my list was to look at the job market in the field of study I was hoping to get into. In my case, it was Human Resource Management. As I researched the market I noticed the demand for HR managers was increasing and it was anticipated to continue growing through 2025. This motivated me to dive into this field with open arms in hopes that opportunities would begin to reveal themselves to me and I could begin building that *normal* life I so desperately wanted.

Had I not prepared these options in advance, the potential for things to have gone left would've been far more certain. Therefore, I offer the following lessons learned:

- Write out a list of things you want to accomplish and look at it daily

- Never put it away and place it where its visible to you

- Try to avoid those you called *friend* before your attempt at a transformation

- Change your circle of friends, find a mentor, and start hanging with like-minded individuals and individuals that will positively challenge you

- Read more books

- Open your mind up to exploring places and things unfamiliar to you

- Open yourself up to more possibilities

These simple steps will open a world of possibilities by expanding your worldview. They say reading is fundamental and I have found this to be true. I mean, think about it, it can't hurt to read about Daymond Garfield John, P. Diddy Combs, Percy Miller "Master P",

Warren Buffet, Russell Simmons, Bill Gates, Steve Jobs, Curtis "50 Cent" Jackson, Richard Branson and others. How did they get to where they are? What motivates them? How do they overcome challenges? What is their recipe for success?

Everyone goes through struggles in one way or another and you'll be surprised at our common emotions, setbacks, challenges and struggles. What better way to overcoming challenges than to read about the way others managed to. You'll notice that you will begin to feel and look at things different and you will possibly no longer fit in with your old crowd. You will also begin to realize that some of the things you were taught over the years were pure fallacy. These new measures and goals will contribute to your lifelong transformation.

Chapter Thirty

REENTRY

I believe felons become accustomed to being told *NO* so much that they give up trying to get ahead. It's time to throw those negative thoughts out and fight for what rights we still have. Trying to figure out what I could and could not do after my felony convictions has been a challenge over the years.

I've heard multiple times from various former inmates, that they couldn't do this or that because they had a felony conviction. I believed what they told me because I heard it so often. No one provided unmistakable evidence to prove or disprove the rumors, not to mention the laws change continuously anyway.

I must admit that for a long time after my first release I pretty much believed everything folks told me as well. The second time around however, I promised myself that following my release, I would conduct my own research to find out the facts.

I clearly remember everyone's excitement when Barak Obama was running for President. We had long hoped an African-American president would eventually lead the land. We also knew that to get him there, every vote would count. One of my friends mentioned to me that he and his wife were going to vote for Obama and how it was a shame that I wouldn't be able to vote in such a historical election. I was like, "Why you say that?" and they were like, "Didn't you just get out of prison? Don't you have a felony conviction?" I was like, "Yes and?" They seemed as if they knew what they were talking about, so I thought, "Damn I need to find out if this is true." I began to research things on the internet and ask relevant people questions on the subject.

I contacted the Department of Voter Registration and found out that a felon indeed loses his/her right to vote once they have been convicted of a crime. However, getting back your right to vote depends on the state you live in. In New York state for example, once you've been released from state custody, meaning from prison, and once you are also free and clear of parole or probation you are once again able to register to vote. Once you register your information, you receive the location of your polling place in the mail. Once received you can vote again. As of April 18, 2018, Governor Cuomo restored the right to vote to all New York State parolees. So now as soon as you're released from prison you no longer must wait to be released from State custody you can vote right away if you are registered.

Another fallacy I heard often was that felons cannot obtain a passport. After applying for a passport of my own, it was time to dispel this fictitious information. Turns out the steps you go through to vote again are the same ones you take in obtaining a passport. To be approved for a passport after a felony conviction, you must be completely released from state custody to include probation and parole. Once this occurs you are free to fill out your application and submit all the necessary documents with your completed application and fees. You must mail your disposition and date of discharge papers in along with your application or the process could be delayed.

Regaining the right to vote and travel abroad, allowed me to feel somewhat normal again and I began to feel empowered and whole. We take our rights and responsibilities for granted until they are taken from us. But knowledge is power, and it is important not to let hearsay dictate how we move forward.

Lastly, I've heard many released prisoners state they would not be able to attend college because of their felony status but this is also not true. When applying for college it is important to be open and honest about your past. When asked if you have been convicted of a felony, simply state yes so it is not discovered later and addressed at another time.

I will say however that acceptance into college programs may depend on the charge itself which then determines whether you will be accepted into the college of your choice. It may also impact whether you will be able to receive federal and state aid. I worked with the financial aid department at the college I was accepted to and they helped me fill out the FASFA forms correctly, so I could obtain extra financial help. I needed support in obtaining the State Pell Grant as well as the Federal Student Aid Grant. Although I was unable to receive Federal Student Aid I was able to receive State Aid. In addition, scholarship money is available, which helped offset the cost of my tuition. People sometimes forget to inquire about available scholarship money so make sure to add that to your list of questions when meeting with your financial aid advisor.

Chapter Thirty-One

THREE STRIKES RULE

With the rise of crack cocaine use and associated crimes, the US Justice Department enacted a new anti-violence strategy In March of 1994. Essentially, a violent crime conviction on top of two previous convictions would result in life in prison. This new law sent shock waves through the community and many previously convicted felons now live in fear. Misinterpretation of the law leads to misunderstandings of the application of such a rule. Many returning citizens live in fear of being in the wrong place at the wrong time or being mistaken for a violent criminal and wrongly convicted to life in prison.

The three-strike rule was appealed in 2012 as data revealed that violent crimes were not necessarily reduced and instead prisons were becoming overcrowded. In some cases, the rule was being enacted following a shoplifting charge or some other misdemeanor. Only the state of California applies the three strikes rule to misdemeanors too, though the law has since been appealed.

One distinction of the three-strike rule at one point was that your 3rd offense must be of the same nature as your first two. Critics of the three-strikes rule point out that three instances of shoplifting can get you the same sentence as that of committing a murder. Doling out long sentences for minor offenses is considered by some as cruel and unusual punishment, which is forbidden by the

Eighth Amendment. You must be convicted of a violent felony which is a federal offense, of which there is an extensive list.

Proposition 36 was enacted to ensure people were not sentenced to 25 to life when their third crime committed was a non-violent offense. In such a case, they are to be prosecuted as though the last offense is a 2nd strike offense. Proposition 36 was enacted in part to resolve the issue of prison overcrowding. Jails became filled with people who were not violent offenders. There are some exceptions however, particularly if the latest felony is a cocaine or heroin based controlled substance charge. If you are charged with Possession with Intent to Distribute, the three-strikes rule may still apply. Also, sex crimes are always considered violent felony crimes.

It should be noted that Bill 2269 was recently introduced by Senator Derrick Simmons, D-Greenville that would prevent a prior felony conviction from being considered if more than 10 years have passed since a person's last conviction.

For more information on the three-strikes rule please see references at the end of this book.

Chapter Thirty-Two

AVOIDING RECIDIVISM

Avoiding the trap of going back to prison is and has always been intensely debated and talked about. In fact, in the US, 80% of people who have been incarcerated return to prison within five years. It can be tough not to fall into the same habits, patterns, and groups you used to hang around with. The reason I believe this is so is because you get comfortable with what you know and who you know. The people you choose to hang around with is the biggest cause of going back to jail. To avoid falling back into old bad habits, you're going to have to do some things, if not everything differently.

One of my church brothers told me to try new and different experiences. Things outside my comfort zone. You never know what your true calling is or what other types of things you may enjoy unless you dare to venture out and try something different. Pray and ask God for guidance and to surround you with those who are meant to be in your life. You will then find supportive people walking along side you in the direction you are supposed to be going.

Also, we need to become more in tune with that still small voice, your gut if you will, so we are able to recognize warnings and signs. I remember many a time where I ignored obvious signs to get out or stay away and eventually paid the price.

161

If there were more programs that aid returning citizens get jobs and get into trade school, it would allow them to legally and successfully take care of themselves and their families. It would help decrease the recidivism rate. Furthering the education process for the incarcerated, would also help them gain viable employment once released. And the jobs they secure would be more apt to pay them a living wage, enough to sustain themselves. Unable to secure a respectable job is one of the reasons a lot of people turn to crime in the first place. Additionally, returning citizens, though well-qualified are not afforded many job opportunities because of their past. This is unfair shows a high rate of discrimination.

A lack of resources and ability to buy the basic needs propels some to find illegal ways to supplement their income. This has and probably will continue to be one of the most overlooked issues. It seems that the system is set up to keep newly released citizens struggling. Things are made to be so difficult that it tends to be easy for them to say, "Fuck It!" And just go back to what they know and consequently to what got them locked up in the first place.

True rehabilitation requires a fair shot be given to newly released citizens, for example matching skill for skill and leaving out the criminal history portion of an application, to ensure they truly have a chance at creating a new life for themselves and their families. If this was the case, we would find more people employed and less people returning to the system because of an illegal choice they had to make so they could feed, clothe, and provide shelter for their family.

Chapter Thirty-Three

ADVICE TO MY YOUNGER SELF

If I could give my younger self some advice it would be to enroll in college right after high school. Learn as much as possible about money; how to save, how money works, and learn ways to make money work for me. I would've also told myself to be mindful of building good credit as it is so easy to screw it up, which can wreak havoc on a person's ability to get ahead. It is extremely difficult to repair your credit and until you do, there are many things that become unattainable. Poor credit scores can prevent you from obtaining a mortgage or getting a low interest rate on a car loan. These days, some employers screen credit scores as an indicator of a person's management skills. I would have reminded myself over and over about the importance of good credit.

I would also broaden the range of careers I aspired towards and set myself up a contingency plan. While in high school I left myself very few options. I had no contingency plan in the event one of my opportunities fell through. Setting small goals and accomplishing those goals would be helpful. Writing everything out and creating a vision board so I could literally see my goals in front of me would have made things more real and I could've clearly seen what I was working towards.

Next, I would inform myself that living a life solely based on street activity would get me nowhere without a

164

concrete plan. I would focus on the goals I should've set for myself. I would've reminded myself that buying fancy cars, material possessions, and spending money frivolously on partying and drinking, would only trap me in the same position I was in. Which meant I was chasing a different high, through money and the lifestyle, leaving me unable to elevate or grow.

Even if I hustled at first, I would've told myself to immediately start investing in something that would offer me a high return and the ability to build a legal business and create a legacy for my family. I would have a transitional plan to help get me out of the game before something bad happened to me. I would've also remined myself that there is no such thing as a retirement fund when it comes to dealing drugs and that the game is meant to be that, a game that has a beginning and an ending: nothing more. Get in and get out!

Lastly, I would tell myself to figure out what my passion is and what drives me. If I figured that out it would be easier for me to focus on a career or business opportunity. Once I figured that out I'd find myself a mentor in that field and get guidance and suggestions. Someone to help bounce ideas off, and someone who's willing to teach me and give helpful advice so I could avoid certain pitfalls. Someone with a proven success rate and the ability to show me what success looks like and instruct me on how to achieve.

Taking these steps would allow for a better chance at succeeding. Finding a mentor would also help with building a positive and productive network which is key. A friend of mine used to always tell me, "Your network is your net worth." Getting acquainted with a group of successful people who push each other to do well and who assist one another in whatever capacity they can, creates a better chance at success for everyone.

Oh yeah and let me not forget to tell myself to persevere through adversity. You must have grit and tenacity to get through life. Anything of any worth is not going to come easy. Bumping my head will happen but quitting is not an option. I would keep nudging myself and telling myself to get back up, brush the dust off, and keep moving forward. Continue to tell myself that every stumbling block is a lesson learned and to figure out another way to accomplish my goal. The growth is in figuring out the next step towards accomplishing the goal. In addition, I would tell myself not to be afraid to travel outside of my comfort zone. Never venturing away from your neighborhood, leaves little room for expanding your horizons. They say you experience growth whenever you feel some discomfort in learning a new skill, performing a new activity or starting a new job.

Research shows that developing a passion for something is a terrific way to build courage and strength. Music, athletics, a hobby, cars, whatever you're into, spend a good amount of time on that passion. It builds character and allows you to express yourself in ways otherwise neglected.

No matter what, and no matter how many times you get knocked down, keep moving forward. In doing so you will eventually succeed and find additional motivation and encouragement thanks to everything you've accomplished. You won't forget what it took to get there, which makes the victory that much sweeter.

As I sit here I reflect on how often I've thought that had I been armed with the information I now know when I was a youngster, I would've had a much easier time of it. I can only imagine the amount of success I could've had. Then I am reminded: the future is yet to come!

Chapter Thirty-Four

LIFE IS A JOURNEY

Life is all about choices. We don't get to choose the country we're born in, nor do we choose the parents we are given. And we certainly don't get to choose how our childhood will look. There comes a time however, where we must make our own choices. Sure, we have had rotten parents and had chaotic lives, but that doesn't mean it must represent the rest of our life.

I believe a lot of us are not armed with the information we need in making the best plans and we are certainly not given very many opportunities. This journey called life is most certainly that; a journey, not a sprint, dash, destination or anything similar. Your life is a voyage that will take you to the end of your days on earth.

God has a plan for you, and it is up to you to find out what it is. Success depends a lot on your attitude towards life and in your ability to get back up and keep it moving. There is always hope. Never give up!

Trying to navigate life through the obstacles, twists, and turns can be a challenge, but if you are anything like me, who was met with a few more challenges than most, it can be debilitating. Especially to those who are not built with that inner strength, grit and perseverance.

I had a breakthrough when I began to see myself on the other side of my current situation. The mind is so powerful that what you envision and think about most will come to fruition. There is a metaphysical attraction at work and if you continuously think negative thoughts, negative outcomes will come your way. On the other hand, if you focus on positive things, positive results come your way. You will then experience things you've only dreamed about. In turn this will make you want to work on your goals even more. This is when you discover the true you. All choices, whether good or bad, have brought you to this point in your life. There's a lot of journey left, seize it, and make the best of it along the way. As I continue to grow and strive to become better than I was the day before, I believe I can inspire others along my path and through life's challenges. We all can, and you never know whose life you might impact along the way.

Life is a journey, pace yourself---you can achieve your goals and dreams despite your past. Learn, read, research, grow, engage in self-reflection, seek counseling, travel, surround yourself with positive people, get spiritually connected, and know your rights and responsibilities.

And in the words of Curtis "50 Cent" Jackson "Outgrow what you were born into. Don't let the limitations of your background reduce the height of your potential." Life is a journey...

Chapter Thirty-Five

WHAT THE FUTURE HOLDS

One can never be certain what the future holds considering life is so full of possibilities and unpredictable circumstances. I am optimistic however, that my life will continue to blossom and that I will flourish despite the challenges I've experienced. In a perfect world my future looks like a fairy tale. I have a happy wife, a family, and a home full of laughter and memorable, pleasurable experiences.

I don't need a big house, or a white picket fence and I'd rather have a large deck with the mammoth of all grills sitting on it ready for use. I would like a fireplace I can sit in front of, read at my leisure, and where I can snuggle up with my wife. I would also like a close-knit family with regular traditions, especially during the holidays. I would love it if we had routine gatherings.

I would also like to be in a place where I am flourishing financially whether in my own business or in human resources, my chosen field of study. I would also like to contribute to and/or assist guys being released from the prison system. I want to assist them in navigating a system where there is little to no assistance from the state. It is really a passion of mine to see everyone flourish. I hate seeing men and woman try so hard to make a better life for themselves only to be met with obstacle after obstacle.

Lastly, waking up every morning feeling useful, experiencing hope and happiness, and having the ability to pass on what I've learned to others, does my heart proud. Not everyone can say they strive to help and be a blessing to others, but ultimately, that is my goal.

RESOURCES

<u>Certificate of Good Conduct:</u>

According the Criminal Justice of NY website, a certificate of good conduct permits a convicted person to obtain housing, jobs, and other services or benefits that may otherwise be unavailable to them. It is applicable to those who've been convicted of more than one crime. The State Board of Parole is the only entity that can issue a Certificate of Good Conduct.

For Certificates of Good Conduct, you must apply to the Department of Corrections and Community Supervision.

http://www.doccs.ny.gov/pdf/DOCCS-CRD-Application_Instructions.pdf

<u>Certificate of Relief from Disabilities:</u>

The purpose of a Certificate of Relief from Disabilities is to show you've turned your life around and to indicate you've been rehabilitated.

To apply for a Certificate of Relief from Disabilities, you should apply to the court that sentenced you. There are some exceptions outlined on the website, so be sure to read the application process carefully.

http://www.criminaljustice.ny.gov/opca/pdfs/certificatesofrelieffromforfeituresanddisabilitiesqanda.pdf.

<u>Firearms:</u>

If you've been convicted of a felony and want information about restoring your firearm rights and privileges you must seek and request relief from the United States Department of Justice, Office of the Pardon Attorney (www.justice.gov/pardon).

Note that, under the law, individuals with certain conviction histories may be ineligible to have their firearm rights restored. Your assigned Parole Officer will review and check all the information you provide. The process will be completed more quickly if you provide complete and accurate information to the best of your ability and are available to the Parole Officer when he or she contacts you.

Three Strikes Rule:

http://www.courts.ca.gov/documents/Three-Strikes-Amendment-Couzens-Bigelow.pdf

Obtaining a Passport:

Obtain your application through the United States Post Office. Fill it out thoroughly and do not lie on it. Obtain a copy of your discharge from parole or probation papers or your disposition from the courts stating your case has been settled and that you are no longer in state custody. When your passport appointment arises, submit the documents with your fee and application or ask where they can be mailed. If your application is not complete it will delay the process of obtaining your passport.

https://www.uspassporthelpguide.com/passport-for-convicted-felon/

Finding Employment:

Increasingly, employers will hire returning citizens as an incentive for tax purposes. Usually the parole or probation department has a list of employers participating in this "program." There are also Job banks that can point you in the direction of viable employment. Also, if you have enrolled and completed college, the Student Services Department usually has leads on employers who are hiring.

Finding a Counselor or Therapist:

Research therapists online in your area. Pick several and give them a call to see if they are accepting new patients and see if they are in our insurance network or accept the type of insurance you have. Once you find one, call and make your intake appointment.

Building a Strong Resume

There are several community resources in helping citizens with resume building. The local unemployment office is a good place to start. They generally offer resume writing classes free of charge and can help prepare you for an interview. Another benefit of taking a resume building course is that you'll have access to a computer, printer, and copier while attending. Remember that volunteer work, certificates of training and part-time work can be listed on a resume.

Applying to College:

Find a college you are interested in and look over the admissions criteria. Figure out if your crime may prevent you from applying, then proceed from there. Once you know if you qualify for admission, fill out the Free Application for Federal Student Aid (FAFSA). When necessary, ask for assistance from the Student Financial Aid Office. Their role is to assist you along the way.

If you had a drug conviction and are wondering whether your conviction meets all criteria allowable to receive Aid, , there is a form available from the Student Financial Aid Office.

Having a drug-related conviction doesn't mean you can't get any money for school. However, any drug-related conviction (felony or misdemeanor), that occurs while you are receiving financial aid makes you no longer eligible. If your conviction came when you were not receiving aid, you can still be eligible for State and Federal Aid depending on the state you live in.

Voting Rights:

To reclaim your right to vote you must re-register to vote once you have been released from prison. If you have any questions you can visit the Board of Elections' website where it outlines the process to register or simply call your local Board of Elections.

https://www.elections.ny.gov/VotingRegister.html

MORE ABOUT THE AUTHOR

Following his release from prison, Terrell Brady attended Bryant & Stratton College where he earned a dual major in Business and Accounting. He was placed on the Dean's list for five consecutive semesters and held a G.P.A. ranging between 3.50 to 4.0. In 2007, Brady received an A.O.S degree in both fields. At Bryant & Stratton College, Brady received the *Accounting Award of Excellence*, as well as the *Who's Who Among Students in American Junior Colleges* recognition.

Terrell completed two significant internships and began several businesses including Brady Management, a lawn care & property management company and became part owner of the Charleston House restaurant.

He also attended the Urban League of Rochester's *Minority & Women Business Development Division Business Planning Workshop Series*, in 2008. Upon completion he attended RIT's Saunders College of Business and received a certificate in *Strategic Marketing in the Virtual World* and later that same year attended the *Enhancing Financial Performance* workshop.

Terrell Brady volunteered at the Board of Cooperative Education Services (BOCES) GED Classes, where he assisted in tutoring young and older adult males in mathematics.

Terrell continued his educational pursuits at Roberts Wesleyan, where for three consecutive semesters, he received Dean's List recognition for academic performance of a 3.50 or higher. In May 2013, Brady graduated with a Bachelor's in Business Administration from Roberts Wesleyan College.

Made in the USA
Middletown, DE
16 May 2019